A Practical Guide to Teaching Design and Technology in the Secondary School

Design and technology requires the development of graphical skills, practical skills and theoretical knowledge and understanding. This practical and accessible workbook is designed to support student-teachers, NQTs and beginning teachers as they develop their teaching skills, and increase their broader knowledge and understanding for teaching design and technology. It also encourages reflection on practice.

A Practical Guide to Teaching Design and Technology in the Secondary School considers the application of subject knowledge in the classroom, and covers each of the main specialist areas: electronics and communications technology (ECT), food technology, materials technology and textiles technology. Topics covered include:

- design and technology in the school curriculum
- the importance of health and safety
- the use of ICT in the teaching of design and technology
- planning lessons
- managing the classroom
- assessment issues
- the integration of literacy, numeracy, citizenship and sustainability into design and technology
- your own professional development.

It contains a wealth of practical activities and materials that provide excellent opportunities to analyse learning and performance. Case studies are also included, as are examples of existing good practice and a range of tried-and-tested strategies. The book has been designed to be written in directly, and thus provides a useful record of progress.

This book complements the textbook *Learning to Teach Design and Technology in the Secondary School* (also published by Routledge), but can also be used equally successfully on its own. It has been designed to be used by student teachers, NQTs and beginning teachers, by themselves or with others, to develop and reinforce their understanding of some of the most important aspects of learning to teach design and technology.

Gwyneth Owen-Jackson is Senior Lecturer on the PGCE Design and Technology course at the Open University, UK.

Routledge Teaching Guides
Series Editors: Susan Capel and Marilyn Leask

These Practical Guides have been designed as companions to **Learning to Teach [Subject] in the Secondary School**. For information on the Routledge Teaching Guides series please visit our website at www.routledge.com/education.

Other titles in the series:

A Practical Guide to Teaching Physical Education in the Secondary School
Edited by Susan Capel, Peter Breckon and Jean O'Neill.

A Practical Guide to Teaching History in the Secondary School
Edited by Martin Hunt

A Practical Guide to Teaching Modern Foreign Languages in the Secondary School
Edited by Norbert Pachler and Ana Redondo

A Practical Guide to Teaching Citizenship in the Secondary School
Edited by Liam Gearon

A Practical Guide to Teaching ICT in the Secondary School
Edited by Steve Kennewell, Andrew Connell, Anthony Edwards, Cathy Wickens and Michael Hammond

A Practical Guide to Teaching Design and Technology in the Secondary School

Edited by
Gwyneth Owen-Jackson

Routledge
Taylor & Francis Group

LONDON AND NEW YORK

First published 2007 by Routledge
2 Park Square, Milton Park, Abingdon, Oxon, OX14 4RN

Simultaneously published in the USA and Canada
by Routledge
270 Madison Ave, New York NY 10016

Routledge is an imprint of the Taylor & Francis Group, an informa business

Transferred to Digital Printing 2010

© 2007 Gwyneth Owen-Jackson

Typeset in Palatino and Frutiger by
Keystroke, 28 High Street, Tettenhall, Wolverhampton

British Library Cataloguing in Publication Data
A catalogue record for this book is available from the British Library

Library of Congress Cataloging in Publication Data
A catalog record for this book has been requested.

ISBN10: 0–415–42369–4 (pbk)
ISBN10: 0–203–96167–4 (ebk)

ISBN13: 978–0–415–42369–4 (pbk)
ISBN13: 978–0–203–96167–4 (ebk)

Contents

List of illustrations

FIGURES

TABLES

Contributors

Frank Banks is Director of the Centre for Research and Development in Teacher Education and Director of Professional Studies in Education at the Open University (OU). After working as a teacher of Technology, Engineering Science and Science, at both secondary and primary levels, he has worked in teacher professional development at all levels at the University of Wales and the Open University and was a Visiting Professor in the School of Engineering and Advanced Technology, Staffordshire University. Frank has acted as a consultant in the professional development of teachers to Egyptian, South African and Argentinian government agencies and for UNESCO and the World Bank. His research interests are in the fields of science and technology education, teacher professional knowledge, and teacher education and development and he has published extensively in these areas.

John Lee is a Senior Lecturer in Design and Technology Education at Sheffield Hallam University where he has worked in Initial Teacher Education since 1991. His current responsibilities include being a research co-ordinator and leading the Regional Support Centre for the CAD/CAM in Schools Initiative at the university. He has extensive experience of planning and delivering Continuing Professional Development (CPD) and In-service training (INSET) opportunities for practising teachers. Prior to this, he had substantial experience of teaching Design and Technology in secondary schools to Head of Department level. His current research interests include the pedagogy of design and teaching strategies for CAD/CAM.

Tim Lewis is Professor of Design and Technology Education at Sheffield Hallam University. His professional experience includes appointments in secondary schools, two as Head of Department, before entering teacher education. Currently, he is responsible for research and academic development in D&T at Sheffield Hallam University. He is a former Chief Examiner for D&T with the Associated Examining Board and currently an external examiner for PGCE and BSc (Hons) degree courses. He is a founder member and trustee of the Design and Technology Association, and a former chair of the Initial Teacher Education Advisory Group. He is a member of the Specialist Schools and Academies Trust engineering expert panel and consultant to the Qualifications and Curriculum Authority and Technology Enhancement Programme. His principal areas of research are D&T pedagogy, electronic and communications (ECT) and vocational education in schools.

Gwyneth Owen-Jackson is Subject Leader for the PGCE in Design and Technology at the Open University. She has worked in initial teacher education for a number of years and was previously a secondary school Design and Technology teacher and Head of Department. She is Chair of the ITE Advisory Group at the Design and Technology Association, a member of the Association's Council of Management and a consultant with the Qualifications and Curriculum Authority. Her research interests include the development of teachers' professional thinking in Design and Technology and the development of education in post-war Bosnia.

John Robson has 24 years' experience of teaching in secondary schools. These have been in both Design and Technology and Art and Design and include substantial periods of working as a post-16 tutor and as Head of Faculty of Design. Most of this experience has been in Derbyshire schools, but includes a period at the Djanogly City Technology College, Nottingham where he was Curriculum Co-ordinator for Art and Design, working across the faculties of Expressive Arts and Maths, Science and Technology. Since 2002, he has been a Senior Lecturer at the Centre for Design and Technology Education, Sheffield Hallam University, with particular responsibility for the one year PGCE. Since joining the Centre he has also become involved in the development of Key Stage 3 project work through links with the Technology Enhancement Programme. His research interests include education for sustainability through design and technology and the Education Unit at *Practical Action*.

Rowan Todd was previously a secondary school Design and Technology teacher and faculty leader and is currently Senior Lecturer in the Centre for Design and Technology Education at Sheffield Hallam University. He has worked in initial teacher education since 1993 and is well known for his contributions to the DATA/DfEE Electronic Communications Technology and CAD/CAM in Schools Initiatives. He has considerable experience in developing and providing continuing professional development opportunities for teachers. His current research interests include the pedagogy of design and teaching strategies for ECT.

Alison Winson has worked in initial teacher training at the University of Worcester for seven years. Her current roles include course tutor for the secondary PGCE in Design and Technology and secondary Graduate Teacher Programme Coordinator. She has also taught on the primary PGCE and undergraduate Design and Technology courses. Previously she taught Design and Technology and was Head of Department. Her research interests include the motivating factors for teaching as a career.

Sue Wood-Griffiths is a course tutor for the secondary PGCE in Design and Technology at the University of Worcester. She has worked in initial teacher education for three years, contributing to both primary and secondary programmes. Prior to this, she was a Design and Technology teacher and Head of Department in schools in the UK, Germany and Thailand. Her research interests include the development of teachers' reflective practice in Design and Technology.

Nigel Zanker has 12 years' experience as Programme Leader for Initial Teacher Training in Design and Technology at Loughborough University. He is an Ofsted Inspector for Design and Technology, ICT and Citizenship and an Accredited Trainer for the Electronics in School Strategy. His principal areas of research are pupils' technology capability in general education and the use of new and emergent technologies in teaching and learning in design education. He has published on ICT education, design education, and curriculum auditing. His professional experience in secondary schools includes posts of responsibility for Science, Technology and curriculum development.

Series Editors' Introduction

This practical and accessible workbook is part of a series of textbooks for student teachers. It complements and extends the popular textbook entitled *Learning to Teach in the Secondary School: A Companion to School Experience*, as well as the subject-specific textbook *Learning to Teach Design and Technology in the Secondary School*. We anticipate that you will want to use this book in conjunction with these other books.

Teaching is rapidly becoming a more research- and evidence-informed profession. We have used research and professional evidence about what makes good practice to underpin the 'Learning to Teach in the Secondary School' series and these practical workbooks. Both the generic and subject-specific books in the series provide theoretical, research and professional evidence-based advice and guidance to support you as you focus on developing aspects of your teaching or your pupils' learning as you progress through your initial teacher education course and beyond.

This book aims to reinforce your understanding of aspects of your teaching, support you in aspects of your development as a teacher and your teaching and enable you to analyse your success as a teacher in maximising pupils' learning by focusing on practical applications. The practical activities in this book can be used in a number of ways. Some activities are designed to be undertaken by you individually, others as a joint task in pairs and yet others as group work working with, for example, other student teachers or a school- or university-based tutor. Your tutor may use the activities with a group of student teachers. The book has been designed so that you can write directly into it.

In England, new ways of working for teachers are being developed through an initiative remodelling the school workforce. This may mean that you have a range of colleagues to support in your classroom. They also provide an additional resource on which you can draw. In any case, you will, of course, need to draw on additional resources to support your development and the *Learning to Teach in the Secondary School, 4th edition* website (http://www.routledge.com/textbooks/0415363926) lists key websites for Scotland, Wales, Northern Ireland and England. For example, key websites relevant to teachers in England include the Teacher Training Resource Bank (www.ttrb.ac.uk). Others include: www.teachernet.gov.uk which is part of the DfES schools web initiative; www.becta.org.uk, which has ICT resources; and www.qca.org.uk which is the Qualifications and Curriculum Authority website.

We do hope that this practical workbook will be useful in supporting your development as a teacher.

Susan Capel
Marilyn Leask
May 2006

Acknowledgements

Thank you to Penny for allowing us to use her photograph in Chapter 9.

Thank you to all the contributors in this book for their interesting chapters, and to Simon Tween for allowing his e-portfolio work to be used in Chapter 13. Thank you to David Barlex for reading a very early draft of Chapter 1, the comments on this were very helpful. Thank you to Jennifer for her practical support, encouragement and patience.

Introduction

This practical workbook is part of a series 'Teaching [Subject] in the Secondary School: A Practical Guide' and it complements the popular textbook entitled *Learning to Teach Design and Technology in the Secondary School* (2007), published by Routledge, and in several chapters you are referred to this text.

This book considers some of the practical issues relevant to the teaching of Design and Technology. The topics covered include:

- the nature and educational value of Design and Technology;
- the development and application of your specific subject knowledge;
- vocational education and its potential for Design and Technology;
- aspects of teaching, including ICT, cross-curricular issues, the importance of the learning environment, managing pupil behaviour and assessment;
- lesson planning for effective teaching and learning;
- your own professional development.

Each chapter includes:

- an introduction to the topic;
- the aims of the chapter;
- information on the topic, supported by reference to research or professional insights from the classroom. This is supported by a range of practical tasks.
- further readings and/or links that provide in-depth reading to supplement the material in this text.

This book covers all four focus areas of Design and Technology and considers relevant classroom issues for each of these. However, whatever your own focus area, you are recommended to read all four chapters as each is different and gives advice and guidance that can be adapted and applied to any area. Graphics/graphic products does not have a separate chapter as this is not a focus area within ITE but should be integrated within each of the areas. If you have a graphics specialism, it is likely that you will also be expected to teach at least one of the four areas identified in this book, so it is hoped that you will find some useful support for your professional development in this book.

Health and safety is an important issue in Design and Technology but this is covered extensively in the companion textbook *Learning to Teach Design and Technology in the Secondary School* (also published by Routledge) (Owen-Jackson 2007), so is not repeated here.

You might be surprised that the chapter on planning has been left almost to the end. This is because good lesson planning draws on a wide range of knowledge, including subject knowledge, knowledge of pupils' learning, curriculum issues, resources, wider school issues and assessment. These topics are covered first, leading you towards a complete lesson plan. However, you will find the chapter on planning useful at any stage in your training as you can skip over the parts that are, at that stage, unfamiliar to you and return to them at a later date. At least you will be aware of the bigger picture.

This book encourages you to take a professional approach to your training and to your work in the classroom. It has been designed to be written in directly and so provides a useful record. It also wants you, and your pupils, to enjoy the learning that takes place. Design and Technology is an interesting and exciting subject, we hope that you – and your pupils – enjoy it.

REFERENCE

Owen-Jackson, G. (2000) *Learning to Teach Design and Technology in the Secondary School*, London: Routledge.

Part 1 Design and Technology in the classroom

Chapter 1   Design and Technology in school

GWYNETH OWEN-JACKSON

INTRODUCTION

There have been discussions about the nature of Design and Technology since its inception in 1988. This is mainly due to the fact that, in educational terms, Design and Technology is relatively new and still evolving; it does not have a long historical tradition like mathematics and is not clearly understood by many people. The ongoing debate signifies a healthy interest in the subject.

As an aspiring Design and Technology teacher, it is important that you consider the nature of the subject, because your perception of the nature of the subject will influence how you teach it. Your perceptions may arise from your own education, the subject of your degree, your employment history or a mixture of these, and they will inform your views on what the subject is about. Do you think it should focus on design, or practical making skills, or computer-based technology? Should it focus on teaching pupils technological knowledge or how to 'do' technology? This chapter will not necessarily give you an answer to the question 'What is the nature of Design and Technology?', rather, it will encourage you to appreciate that there are likely to be different responses to the question and to reflect on your own current thinking and response.

By the end of this chapter you should be able to:

- define your own understanding of the aims and purposes of Design and Technology;
- justify the place of Design and Technology in the school curriculum.

DESIGN AND TECHNOLOGY IN THE SCHOOL CURRICULUM

The term 'Design and Technology' arose from the first Interim Report published by the Working Group set up by the government to define the subject, and its programme of study, for the National Curriculum (DES/WO 1988). The Interim Report stated that 'Design and Technology' was to be regarded as a 'unitary concept', that there was an 'intimate connection' between the two aspects and that together they created 'a concept which is broader than either design or technology individually' (ibid., p. 2).

The Report further identified the unique contribution that Design and Technology would make to pupils' learning. It stated that the subject would allow pupils to develop the 'capability to operate effectively and creatively in the made world' and that knowledge was to be seen as a resource to be used, that it would become 'active by being integrated into the imagining, decision-making, modelling, making, evaluating and other processes which constitute design and technological activity' (ibid., pp. 29–30). The final report of the Working

Group (DES/WO 1989) confirmed that 'the capability to investigate, design, make and appraise is as important as the acquisition of knowledge' (ibid., p. 1).

It is this foundation which remains at the heart of school-based Design and Technology. The subject is constructed as a 'process' through which pupils learn a range of skills, for example, how to analyse existing products, ways to improve and develop products and how to manipulate materials to produce new products. In order to be able to undertake these processes, they need to learn some knowledge, for example, an understanding of the properties of materials, knowledge about how to cut, join and finish materials, how to collect and analyse data, and strategies for designing – but they acquire this information in order to be able to carry out the process, not for its own sake. It is this that makes Design and Technology different from other curriculum subjects.

The knowledge that pupils develop, though, is not uniquely 'design and technology knowledge'. Pupils will draw on knowledge that relates to Design and Technology, such as the characteristics of materials and manufacturing processes, but will also draw on knowledge from other disciplines, for example, physics, biology, mathematics, art, sociology, as pupils gather together information that they need in order to solve their particular problem with their particular solution.

The contribution that Design and Technology makes to pupils' learning is that it allows them to work both intellectually and practically; it helps them to develop knowledge and then apply that knowledge in a practical task, or to develop knowledge or understanding through engaging in practical activity.

Design and Technology can engage pupils, it is purposeful and it acknowledges pupils' own creativity and responsibility. While others may not see this, as Design and Technology teachers, we need to understand the aims of the subject, and be able to articulate the valuable contribution that it makes to pupils' development.

Activity 1.1 Design and Technology in the school curriculum

Obtain a copy of the National Curriculum programme of study for Design and Technology, either from your training provider, school or the NC website: nc.net.uk Read through the programme of study and list the content under the two headings in the table on p. 6.

THE AIMS AND PURPOSES OF DESIGN AND TECHNOLOGY

The development of Design and Technology as a subject means that it is taught in school by teachers from different disciplines, each of whom brings a different perspective to the subject.

The literature reveals that different meanings are attached to 'design and technology' and these different meanings are often linked to the perceived aims of the subject, which in turn are linked to different values held by the writers. Teachers may consider Design and Technology to be a 'competence-based' subject, teaching pupils how things work and how to carry out practical tasks. Others may see it as preparing young people for work, yet others may see it as a way of helping pupils develop their knowledge and understanding of themselves. These different views will be held by teachers whom you meet and work with and their different views will influence the way in which they teach the subject. For example, if you think the main purpose of Design and Technology is to develop design skills or practical skills, then you will focus on those, alternatively if you perceive it as preparing pupils for work, then you will emphasise other knowledge, skills and ways of working.

Activity 1.1 *continued*

Processes to be taught	Content to be taught

Activity 1.2 The nature of Design and Technology

First of all, think about your own perspective of Design and Technology and complete as much as you can of the following table. Then, if you have the opportunity, talk to other student teachers and record their perspective. Finally, talk to your mentor and other teachers in school to find out their views and record these.

Activity 1.2 *continued*

Design and Technology includes a study of: (list below the knowledge and skills that you consider make up Design and Technology)	This contributes to pupils' learning: (for the knowledge and skills identified, consider what pupils learn from the topic or activity)

Were there differences in the views of different groups, or individuals within the groups? What might account for these differences?

THE CHANGING NATURE OF DESIGN AND TECHNOLOGY

Having considered the nature of the subject and its contribution to pupils' learning, it is also important to recognise that how these are developed is constantly changing. This is because Design and Technology deals with products, materials, tools and processes and, as these develop, so the subject develops in order to remain relevant.

Hughes (2005) talked to classroom teachers and identified the range of changes that have taken place; these related to government policies and examination curricula as well as the introduction of new materials and new processes, all of which have had an impact on the teaching of Design and Technology. In his conclusion, Hughes (ibid., p. 113) states, 'continuous change is inevitable in today's society' and that Design and Technology teachers need to 'constantly adapt and respond to change in a creative and innovative way' (ibid.).

Some of the changes in the past five years include the introduction of the Key Stage 3 National Strategy Framework for Design and Technology with its emphasis on improving the teaching of design skills. This has led some teachers to reconsider what and how they teach when asking pupils to 'design'. The introduction of a GCSE in Product Design, which brings together work in the different focus areas, is another new development. Developments in materials have seen the introduction of more affordable 'smart' and modern materials into schools, for example, polymorph, thermocolour sheets and modified starches. Developments in ICT and software have seen more schools using CAD/CAM systems and rapid prototyping.

More recently there have been concerns over the place of creativity in Design and Technology – how do we recognise it?, how do we foster and encourage it?, how do we assess it? Issues of sustainability are also coming to the fore – what is the role of Design and Technology in increasing pupils' awareness of the environmental, economic and social consequences of designing and making?

Activity 1.3 The changing nature of Design and Technology

In the table below, Design and Technology teachers have listed what they were taught in the subject some years ago. In the middle column, list what you were taught in the curriculum area of 'design and technology', whatever label was used for the subject. In the final column, list what is taught today, you will find this either from schools you visit, Awarding Body websites or up-to-date textbooks.

What was taught 20–30 years ago	What you were taught	What is taught today
Materials used: 'CDT' Plywood Pine Food Basic foods: flour, eggs, sugar, fruit, vegetables, meat, cheese – all fresh foods		
Tools/equipment used: 'CDT' Steel rule Try square Hand saws, different types Hand drill		

Activity 1.3 *continued*

Food Basic hand equipment Bowls Wooden spoons Gas/electric cookers		
Processes learnt: 'CDT' Measuring Cutting Drilling Making wood joints Sanding Food Rubbing in Making pastry Cake-making methods Fruit/vegetable preparation Making family meals Topics covered: 'CDT' Food Fruit crumble Rock buns Stuffed jacket potatoes Meat pie		

When you have completed the table, answer the following questions:

- What do these lists tell you about the changing nature of Design and Technology?

- What were the periods of major change?

- What are your views on these changes?

Design and Technology in schools today is likely to draw on a similar range of materials and equipment but with the addition of modern and smart materials and, where possible, the use of industry-standard equipment. There is likely to be much more use of ICT and pupils are much more likely to be encouraged to be actively engaged in developing their own work and making their own decisions.

However, change is constant and it's likely that the next few years will see developments in pupils' use of new technologies, more emphasis on values in pupils' work and more attention paid to the development of pupils' creativity and innovation. This does not mean that the essential nature of the subject will change but that teachers' classroom practice will evolve to ensure that the subject remains relevant to pupils.

SUMMARY

This chapter has considered the nature of Design and Technology, and shown that this remains the same even though the content of the subject is constantly changing. You have been encouraged to think about your own view of Design and Technology and its aims.

The discussions about the nature and purpose of Design and Technology are likely to continue due to its organic nature. In these discussions there is always likely to be a variety of opinions and it is important that you begin to think through where you stand on these issues in order to be able to contribute meaningfully to the discussion.

REFERENCES

DES/WO (1988) *Interim Report of the Working Group for Design and Technology*, London: DES
DES/WO (1989) *Design and Technology for Ages 5 to 16: Proposals of the Secretary of State for Education and Science and Secretary of State for Wales*, London: DES
Hughes, C. (2005) 'Managing change in design and technology', in E.W.L. Norman, D. Spendlove and P. Grover (eds) *Inspire and Education: DATA International Research Conference 2005*, Wellesbourne: DATA

FURTHER READING

Kimbell, R., Stables, K. and Green, R. (1996) *Understanding Practice in Design and Technology*, Buckingham: Open University Press. Chapter 2 discusses what 'technology' is and Chapter 3 looks at Design and Technology in schools.
McCormick, R. (2002) 'The coming of technology education in England and Wales', in G. Owen-Jackson (ed.) *Teaching Design and Technology in Secondary Schools: A Reader*, London: RoutledgeFalmer.
Sayers, S., Morley, J. and Barnes, B. (eds) (2002) *Issues in Design and Technology Teaching*, London: RoutledgeFalmer. Chapter 1 gives an overview of the development of Design and Technology in schools.

WEBSITES

www.data.org
This is the website of the Design and Technology Association, the professional association for teachers, which provides up-to-date information and details of courses and conferences.

www.secondarydandt.org
This website is run by the Nuffield Foundation and provides up-to-date information about developments in the subject.

Chapter 2

Electronics and Communications Technology (ECT) in the classroom

JOHN LEE AND ROWAN TODD

INTRODUCTION

In *Learning to Teach Design and Technology in the Secondary School* (Owen-Jackson 2007) published by Routledge, Chapter 4 considers the subject knowledge required to teach control and systems. Since the publication of that book, this area of the Design and Technology curriculum has increasingly become known as 'electronics and communications technology' (ECT) to reflect the huge growth in telecommunications and information technology, and the original text has been revised to take account of these developments. In this chapter we have provided an up-dated ECT subject knowledge audit.

ECT encompasses the whole range of electronic products and services that make up the technological infrastructure of a modern society. Whether at home, work or play, these electronic systems, products and services are at the heart of many aspects of modern life. Education is vital in helping pupils to understand and interact effectively with these new technologies and Design and Technology makes a key contribution to this by providing a wealth of opportunities to study the principles of ECT and apply these in a practical context.

This chapter will provide you with an insight into the scope and nature of ECT in the contemporary school curriculum and enable you to monitor your personal capability in this area, investigate a range of teaching strategies and resources and explore further training opportunities.

By the end of this chapter you should be able to:

- be aware of the knowledge and skills required to teach ECT;
- broaden your personal awareness of key ideas and concepts in the ECT curriculum;
- explore curriculum development opportunities and pedagogic issues in ECT;
- investigate strategies and resources for delivering ECT-based project activity.

SKILLS, KNOWLEDGE AND UNDERSTANDING IN THE ECT CURRICULUM

During the initial phase of your training, you will have become familiar with a range of materials that identify the key competences required to teach ECT, for example, the National Curriculum (DfEE/QCA 1999), the DATA minimum competences (DATA 2003) and public examination specifications all make references to key aspects of knowledge, skills and understanding in ECT.

The Design and Technology Association paper, *Minimum Competences for Trainees to Teach Design and Technology in Secondary Schools* (2003), identifies the ECT subject knowledge required to teach to Key Stage 3 (Tier 1) and Key Stage 4 and beyond (Tier 2). Whatever your present capability, if you intend to teach ECT you will need to explore the content of the ECT curriculum in the school context and reflect on your own ability to teach it. Carrying out the audit outlined in Activity 2.1 will enable you to do both of these things.

Activity 2.1 Auditing your ECT subject knowledge

Use the following as a basis for monitoring your progress at key points during your training.

Use this audit to monitor the development of your subject knowledge in ECT. We have identified the start of your teacher training, the mid-point and the end of your training as key points but you can change these to suit your own circumstances. Enter the following to indicate your level of capability in each category:

- S – a particular area of strength
- C – competent in this area
- D – an area for development.

Note: If you are intending to become a specialist teacher of ECT, it is the competences required to teach to Tiers 1 and 2 which should be your guide. If you expect to teach ECT to Key Stage 3 only, then you need to consider Tier 1.

As a newly qualified teacher you should be able to:

Designing

Tier 1

	Start of ITT	mid-point review	End of ITT
Make creative use of commercial electronic modules when designing products in other material areas (*e.g. sound modules, digital sound recorders, radio modules*);			
Understand and use a systems approach when designing with electronics;			
Understand and be able to use graphical computer control languages to design control solutions;			
Use appropriate computer software to design and model simple electronic circuits using a systems approach;			
Design simple mechanical solutions incorporating cams, levers, gears and pulleys;			

Tier 2

	Start of ITT	mid-point review	End of ITT
Develop control systems through the interconnection of a range of kits, components and subsystems;			
Be able to use control programming languages to develop efficient control solutions;			
Use software to design, model and analyse electronic circuits;			

Activity 2.1 *continued*

Analyse the design of mechanical, electrical and electronic products in terms of their intended users, the design features that suit them to these users and their technical operation at a systems level;

Make use of their technical understandings of components and systems to analyse and describe the operation of mechanical, electrical and electronic products;

Recognise that the development of new technologies creates product design opportunities and be confident in citing examples (e.g. Lithium polymer batteries for smaller mobile phones, MP3 technology for new portable entertainment devices, flash-card storage media for digital cameras);

Display an understanding of expected future developments in electronics and communication technologies and convey these clearly (e.g. new consumer products brought about by the 'digital revolution', embedded computer technology to produce 'smart' products, the convergence of information systems via network technologies);

Produce and interpret simple circuit diagrams using correct British Standard symbols; produce and interpret systems diagrams; produce and interpret flow charts; use simple formulae to communicate principles and concepts;

Create and interpret system construction and functional information and communicate it by means of circuit diagrams, flowcharts, systems diagrams, truth tables, graphs, tables, appropriate formulae and mechanical diagrams;

Present and interpret data on system, module or component function;

Use sophisticated data to inform the design of products including mechanical, electrical and electronic elements;

Develop clear user instructions for control systems.

Develop appropriate user interfaces for control systems (e.g. the adjustment direction of a potentiometer, switch position and labelling, user feedback from sounders, optical indicators and displays);

Create and interpret clear and precise manufacturing information for control systems.

Making

Tier 1

Tier 2

Systematically construct and test simple circuits using stripboard and/or printed circuit board;

Model and test system building blocks making effective use of system modelling techniques (e.g. breadboarding; computer simulation);

Use a computer and interface box, or microcontroller module, with appropriate electronic sensors and actuators;

Understand how computers, microcontrollers and electronic circuits can be used to control a range of actuators (e.g. electrical, mechanical, hydraulic, pneumatic);

Use appropriate computer software to design and make printed circuit boards (PCBs);

Use software to support the design of PCBs that are well matched to product casing and take into account the need for circuit testing;

Activity 2.1 *continued*

Prototype simple mechanical solutions incorporating cams, levers, gears and pulleys using both made and bought elements;

Analyse the manufacture of a range of mechanical, electrical and electronic products in terms of how the manufacturing processes and materials enable production at an appropriate scale and cost.

Use systems-based understanding to check the operation of a manufactured circuit.

Describe the advanced manufacturing industrial technologies used to manufacture modern mass-produced consumer electronic products (e.g. surface mounting techniques, automated assembly, rapid prototyping, injection moulding);

Analyse the performance of systems in order to check that they are working effectively, using a range of appropriate test equipment (e.g. multimeter, logic probe, oscilloscope).

Knowledge and Understanding

Tier 1

Understand that mechanical, electrical and electronic systems can be interconnected to achieve different purposes;

Describe feedback as a signal loop in a system diagram and understand how it is used in control systems to ensure that operations are achieved successfully (e.g. limit switches);

Understand the use of potential divider circuits with sensors and use them in switching circuits;

Understand that data can be transferred across a distance both with and without wires;

Use programming software to control simple products;

Use programming software to program a microcontroller for simple stand-alone control;

Use truth tables to describe and solve simple logic problems;

Tier 2

Understand the requirements for interfacing between subsystems as well as to sensors and actuators (e.g. signal matching, simple analogue to digital conversion);

Use systems diagrams and flowcharts appropriately to describe the operation of continuous and sequential control systems;

Understand the operation of a wide range of sensors and actuators and use this knowledge to make considered judgements in selecting appropriate components for a design situation; understand the principles of use of an appropriate range of electrical and electronic components including integrated circuits (ICs);

Understand the principles of use of a range of techniques for transferring data between control systems separated by a distance (e.g. infra-red, radio, coding systems);

Use programming software to produce sophisticated systems that are able to control and respond to a wide range of external devices;

Incorporate programmable devices into control solutions (e.g. PIC-based microcontrollers);

Use truth tables to analyse and design logic systems;

Activity 2.1 *continued*

Understand the use of resistors and determine their values using the colour code; understand the basic units of electricity and use the resistance equation to calculate current, voltage and resistance within a variety of circuits;		
Appreciate the need for and requirements of structures in the construction of mechanical and electromechanical systems;		
Describe a range of simple mechanical devices and drive systems;		
Describe the forms of mechanical movement and the use of mechanisms to translate between them;		
Discuss the social and environmental consequence of using new technologies.		

Use appropriate equations to support the design and analysis of electrical, electronic and mechanical control systems (e.g. formulae for power, potential dividers, amplifier gain, simple and compound gear systems, pulleys, levers);		
Understand the principles of use of an appropriate range of mechanisms, including considerations of power transfer (e.g. simple and compound gear trains, pulley systems, cams);		
Describe the social and environmental impacts of a range of products and manufacturing systems (e.g. improved mass communication and the possible health risks of using mobile phones, the environmental consequences of disposable batteries);		
Apply appropriate technical principles and concepts in the analysis of the function of a range of mechanical, electrical and electronic products.		

Source: Adapted from DATA (2003).

EXPLORING OPPORTUNITIES TO DEVELOP YOUR ECT CAPABILITY

If you have identified some gaps in your knowledge and skills, there are several ways in which you could develop these. There may be opportunities to develop your subject knowledge during your initial training; many courses offer core modules or electives where the key skills and concepts of ECT can be studied in some depth. These can be enhanced by the use of self-directed learning opportunities to focus in more depth on particular aspects of ECT where possible.

During school placements explore opportunities to become directly involved with the teaching of ECT as this will enable you to observe and work with experienced members of staff and give you an insight into effective teaching and learning strategies and resource management issues.

TEACHING AND LEARNING IN ECT

Such is the complexity of many electronic systems, products and services that it would be easy for pupils to feel overawed at the prospect of trying to understand how they work. In reality, many technological systems can be broken down into more readily understandable sub-systems that can function and be tested independently in what is often referred to as a 'systems' approach. Effective teaching and learning take place when pupils use the 'systems' approach to learn the core concepts and skills of ECT and are given the opportunity to apply these in the design and manufacture of quality electronic products. You need to consider in your teaching how to help pupils overcome the difficulties they may face in ECT and how you can maximise their learning. Activity 2.2 will help you to understand some of the issues that need to be addressed.

Activity 2.2 Curriculum implementation/support

Choose an ECT project that you have taught, or observed being taught in your placement school or place of work, and use it to complete the following.

Using the ECT project that you have selected, consider the project in detail and describe it using the following headings:

Project description:
Note the key ideas or concepts that were covered, think about what pupils learnt not just what they made.

Year group:
Previous ECT experience of the group:

Supporting resources:
Note the practical equipment, textbooks, videos and other resources available.

Teaching issues:
Describe, for example, teaching methods used; relative timings; range of different activities; how resources were organised.

Pupil activity:
Describe, for example, activities that developed pupils' knowledge, skills and understanding; what the pupils designed and made, how they worked.

Learning outcomes:
Describe, for example, what the pupils gained from engaging in this activity – you should focus on the learning outcomes rather than what the pupils made.

Activity 2.2 *continued*

Now consider the following questions, in relation to this project:

Are there any areas that caused problems for pupils?

Had they all undertaken the prior learning required?

Were there any key concepts that they found difficult?

Could they access and use all the resources?

Was consideration given to economic, moral and social issues as well as subject knowledge?

Are there any gaps in your own subject knowledge that need to be addressed before you could teach this project?

Think about your responses to the questions, if you have identified any issues that you need to develop, you will find it helpful to talk to your mentor or tutor about these before you begin to plan your own teaching.

You could repeat this task for all the schemes of work across a Key Stage; this would allow you to see how pupils' knowledge and skills in ECT are developed through the planned learning activities. It will also be useful for you to consider using this format when planning your own sequences of lessons as it will be a helpful guide.

ECT can be taught through a range of projects that will appeal to pupils, for example, developing a tooth-brushing timer or a nail-polish drying timer; animated patches to add to clothing; rainfall monitors; sweet dispensers. Most projects incorporate the use of software and many include other aspects of Design and Technology, for example, designing and graphic skills and making casings from resistant materials or textiles.

Designing in ECT has two aspects: (1) the designing of electronic circuits or systems; and (2) designing a suitable casing. Circuit design is often done with software packages, these allow pupils to design and test circuits before building them. Casing or housing units are

17

designed to hold the circuits and so have a number of constraints that must be taken into account. In some schools, ECT and materials technology are integrated so that pupils can develop and draw on ECT and/or materials technology knowledge and skills as appropriate.

In the classroom, you will be required to manage both pupils' learning and the resources (see Chapter 10 in this book for guidance on managing pupils in the classroom). We discuss ECT resources below; in the classroom you will need to:

- ensure there are sufficient resources for the work you plan;
- find out how resources are ordered in your school, is this through the technician, head of department or the classroom teacher?;
- consider how resources will be distributed to pupils – will you hand them out, will they collect their own?;
- consider how resources will be collected in at the end of the lesson – ensure you allow sufficient time for this and make sure that you count in resources to ensure that all are returned.

Chapter 5 in this book contains advice on managing small equipment in textiles technology, this could equally be applied to ECT resources.

RESOURCING ECT

Resources to support effective teaching and learning in ECT are developing rapidly with computers and online resources increasingly featuring in classrooms. ICT is an almost integral part of ECT and teachers and pupils have access to components, processes and systems that more accurately reflect developments in the wider world, for example, by using Peripheral Interface Control (PIC) chip technology, pupils can now manufacture with relative ease, and at minimal cost, products that have in-built control systems. There is a rapidly growing range of commercial resources available that are specifically designed to support project-based learning in ECT, including, for example, circuit design and simulation software.

The combination of innovative teaching strategies and exciting contexts, supported by high quality teaching resources, is creating learning environments in ECT that provide challenging and motivating experiences, encourage self-directed learning and enable pupils to study at their own pace. Activity 2.3 offers you the opportunity to explore and evaluate the resources that are available to support the teaching of ECT.

Activity 2.3 Identifying the ideal ECT facility

Note: In preparation for this task, if possible, visit a school that has been identified as succeeding with the teaching of electronics. Take the opportunity to talk to teachers and pupils about aspects of their work and look at project outcomes and resource provision.

- Identify the resources you think would contribute to creating an ideal learning environment for a flexible and dynamic ECT curriculum at Key Stage 3. These may be resources currently in your school or the school you visit, or may be resources that you, your mentor or tutor think would add to pupils' learning experience.
- Complete the table to provide you with a record of these resources. Record any comments on the value or purpose of the resource.

Activity 2.3 *continued*

Hardware	Software	Consumables	Teaching resources	Other
e.g. interactive whiteboard	e.g. pic simulation package	e.g. PCB developer and etchant	e.g. appropriate videos/DVDs	e.g. task-specific lighting

CURRICULUM SUPPORT: THE ELECTRONICS IN SCHOOLS STRATEGY

The Electronics in Schools Strategy (EiSS) has been developed with the overarching aim of encouraging more young people to become interested in the study of ECT. The initiative is designed to raise standards in teaching and learning in electronics by:

- engaging more pupils in learning about electronics and its applications;
- enhancing teacher expertise through the provision of high quality continuing professional development;
- providing access to quality resources;
- encouraging progression in the secondary age phase.

The EiSS offers various opportunities for training and support. The ECT in Schools website (www.marconiect.org) also provides access to a dedicated training resource and in-depth support material, designed to assist in the promotion, teaching and delivery of ECT within the school curriculum.

For those of you wishing to specialise in this area, accreditation through the EiSS electronics training programme may be a possibility. Activity 2.4 will provide you with more information on this and other aspects of the initiative.

Activity 2.4 Accessing online curriculum support for ECT

Obtain access to the ECT in Schools website (www.marconiect.org) which is designed to provide support and guidance for teachers of electronics. Explore the website, paying particular attention to the sections headed:

- Why teach electronics?
- Training
- School Case Studies
- Project Case Studies

SUMMARY

In this chapter you have been introduced to the scope and nature of the emerging ECT curriculum and the unique opportunities that this presents for pupils in the secondary age phase. New opportunities, developments in software and a host of new and exciting components and materials now make the subject more accessible and relevant to the pupils of today.

Introducing pupils to the technological world in which they live through exciting, hands-on project work can be very rewarding. As a developing area of the Design and Technology curriculum, ECT offers excellent opportunities for you as a newly qualified teacher.

REFERENCES

DATA (2003) *Minimum Competences for Trainees to Teach Design and Technology in Secondary Schools*, Research Paper 4, Wellesbourne: DATA

DfEE/QCA (1999) *Design and Technology Key Stages 1 to 4*, London: HMSO

Owen-Jackson, G. (2000) *Learning to Teach Design and Technology in the Secondary School*, London: Routledge.

WEBSITES

www.data.org.uk
www.marconiect.org
This website supports the Electronics in Schools Strategy and provides a range of useful information.

Chapter 3   Food technology in the classroom

GWYNETH OWEN-JACKSON

INTRODUCTION

Food programmes appear regularly on television and are increasingly popular but many people know surprisingly little about food. Food technology can make an important contribution to pupils' learning in Design and Technology as it allows them to learn and develop knowledge and skills using 'materials and components' with which they are familiar. The National Curriculum (DfEE/QCA 1999) identifies that the importance of Design and Technology rests on the belief that it allows pupils to 'think and intervene creatively to improve quality of life', to 'look for needs, wants and opportunities and respond to them' and to 'combine practical skills with an understanding of aesthetics, social and environmental issues, function and industrial practices' – all of these can be achieved through the medium of food.

This chapter considers what is taught in food technology in the school curriculum and how this continues to develop, as well as some of the practical issues involved. It also looks at the contribution that food technology makes to pupils' learning of the wider aspects of the school curriculum.

By the end of this chapter you should:

- be aware of the subject knowledge for teaching food technology;
- know what is covered in food technology in the school curriculum;
- have considered some of the practical issues in teaching food technology;
- be aware of food technology's contribution to the wider school curriculum;
- be aware of resources available to food technology teachers.

FOOD TECHNOLOGY WITHIN DESIGN AND TECHNOLOGY

Food technology covers the designing and making of food products and requires pupils to learn about nutrition, food science, making processes and food manufacturing, including health and hygiene, quality assurance and food product development. In order to be able to teach food technology effectively, you need to have a range of knowledge and skills; in *Learning to Teach Design and Technology in the Secondary School* (Owen-Jackson 2007), there is detailed consideration of the knowledge required and lists against which you can audit your own knowledge and skills (this text is currently under revision to reflect developments in subject knowledge). The Design and Technology Association have now updated the recommended minimum competences to take account of developments, for example, the increasing use of modern and smart food ingredients, and you are advised to obtain a copy of these (DATA 2003).

As with all areas of Design and Technology, food technology is constantly developing; Bielby (2005) notes that industrial food production develops as technologies develop and this requires food technology teachers to keep their own subject knowledge up to date. This can be done in a number of ways, for example, reading literature from the food industry, accessing food industry websites, reading relevant teaching materials (such as those produced by the Meat Marketing Board or the British Nutrition Foundation), attending courses and learning from colleagues. Some teachers have also been able to establish links with local food manufacturers and developed their knowledge through arranging visits and work placements. The Further Reading at the end of this chapter provides some guidance on textbooks and websites.

Designing with food

One aspect of Design and Technology that has proved difficult to locate in food technology has been that of 'design' (see Rutland *et al.* 2005). Designing, as practised in other focus areas, is less obvious in food technology and Rutland *et al.* (ibid., p. 159) point out that food technology teachers need to establish 'an agreed vocabulary to describe the design decisions' that pupils make in food technology. I would suggest that we begin by describing what occurs in food technology as 'food product development', a term used in industry and one that better describes designing in food.

Some of the designing strategies used in other focus areas, however, can be adapted for food product development and many teachers are using activities from the National Strategy materials for Design and Technology (DfES 2004). It is important to remember, though, that it is unlikely that pupils will need to draw their food product ideas; they will illustrate ideas through amended recipes, nutritional or costing analyses and through modelling (practical making). For example, in one school the scheme of work begins with product analysis, pupils consider 'layered' sweet products and think about whether the pastry, filling or topping could be amended. They then use these thoughts as a basis for new product ideas and spend some time researching nutrition and costs and making some of their ideas to test for flavour, texture and appearance. Sketches may be used occasionally to illustrate a concept or for packaging design.

Activity 3.1 Food product development activities

Complete the table on p. 23 to help you evaluate existing food product development activities in your school. For each year group in Key Stage 3, select one design and make activity in food technology and record how pupils are asked to carry out the 'design' part of the work.

You will find some guidance on general design strategies in the National Strategy materials for Design and Technology (DfES 2004), and some of these can be adapted for food. You will also find ideas on the Food Forum website (see web addresses at the end of this chapter).

Product analysis

Product analysis can be used at various points in pupils' work. At the beginning, existing products can be analysed before pupils begin their own product development. At the end, it could be used to analyse pupils' own products. However, as with any teaching, you should consider carefully the purpose of using product analysis and match the activity to the intended learning.

Activity 3.1 *continued*

Year group	Design and make activity title	Food product development activities
7		
8		
9		

Now consider the following questions:

How much variety is there in what pupils are asked to do?

How effective are these 'design' activities? How well do they help the pupils develop new food product ideas?

Does their food product development work include using ICT to model nutritional aspects of dishes, changing the ratio of ingredients, or change ingredients to affect the cost?

Can you plan alternative ways for pupils to develop ideas for food products?

Product analysis includes a wide range of activities, including:

- *Visual analysis* – what the product looks like: its colour, shape, size and presentation;
- *Textual analysis* – this can be done by pupils breaking or eating products to describe their texture or scientifically, for example, to test breaking point or 'shortness' using weights;
- *Taste* – pupils should be encouraged to taste a range of new and different foods and analyse them using an appropriate range of vocabulary; word banks are helpful here, as is modelling by the teacher to show how taste analysis should be done.

Sensory analysis can be undertaken for taste or for all the above elements. If undertaken, this should be done as scientifically as possible with consideration given to the presentation of the foods to be tested, water for cleaning the palate between tasting and proper recording of the results. There is some guidance on sensory evaluation tests in Owen-Jackson (2001).

Food technology knowledge and skills

In addition to product development, pupils need opportunities to develop their practical making skills, knowledge and practical application of hygiene and safety, knowledge and understanding of nutritional and scientific aspects of foods and how these link to product development, marketing aspects of food production and the social, cultural and environmental influences. Activity 3.3 helps you understand how knowledge and skills are developed across Key Stage 3 in your school.

Activity 3.2   Product analysis

Plan a product analysis activity for a class you know. Use the lesson pro-forma provided by your school or training provider. Decide what the purpose of the product analysis is to be and plan appropriate activities. Think about:

- Whether you need to provide products or, if pupils are to make them, do you need to provide ingredients?
- Will pupils work individually or in groups?
- What kind of analysis tests will they undertake – do they need any equipment for this?
- How will they record the results?
- What will the follow-up activity be?

Activity 3.3   Reviewing schemes of work

Look again at the schemes of work for Key Stage 3 food technology in your school. Read carefully all the schemes and answer the questions below.

From the schemes of work for Key Stage 3 food technology in your school, answer the following questions:

- What is the balance of practical and written work – do pupils engage frequently in practical work?

- Do pupils' practical skills develop so that they learn more complex skills?

- Are pupils supported to make good quality products that will be eaten?

- Do pupils develop good nutritional knowledge?

- Do pupils develop knowledge and understanding of hygienic practices?

- Are pupils encouraged to develop subject-specific vocabulary?

- Do pupils learn about the scientific properties of ingredients and how these are applied in food products?

Activity 3.3 *continued*

- Do pupils know and use quality assurance procedures?

- Do pupils develop knowledge of food industry practices?

- Are economic issues addressed?

- Are moral and environmental issues addressed?

- Are pupils made aware of social and cultural influences on food products?

- Do pupils develop good evaluative skills?

- Is there any cross-curricular learning, for example, are the literacy and numeracy skills made explicit? is ICT used to develop pupils' learning?

- Do Year 7 schemes of work take account of learning in the primary school?

- Does the learning include increasing complexity and challenges for pupils as they move into Year 8 and Year 9?

- Do the schemes have progression so that pupils' knowledge and skills develop in coherent way across the Key Stage?

There are a lot of questions to answer, but the information you obtain will help you to see how pupils' knowledge and skills are developed over the Key Stage. When you have completed the activity, depending on your answers, consider whether there are ways in which the schemes of work could be amended to improve pupils' learning. For example, do they consider sufficiently the subject-specific vocabulary, and are there opportunities to develop more complex practical skills?

Ofsted (2006) have identified that effective teaching of food technology occurs when pupils engage in frequent practical activities, whether this be cooking dishes or undertaking experimental work. They also acknowledged, however, that there are some practical constraints which can hinder pupils' development in food technology.

PRACTICAL ISSUES IN FOOD TECHNOLOGY

There are a range of constraints in some schools; these include limited space for teaching, large class sizes, lack of equipment, short lesson times. Whether these are present in your school or not, the nature of food technology means that lessons need to be planned carefully and in detail. Below we outline some of the main considerations.

Food ingredients

The main issue with ingredients is whether these are supplied by the school or brought in by pupils. In the majority of schools, pupils will provide their own ingredients for practical lessons; this raises a number of questions:

- Does the socio-economic context of your school influence what pupils learn, for example, do you/do pupils only choose products that they can afford rather than those that would support their learning?
- Does it limit experimental or investigative work – do pupils always have to cook food that they can take home?
- Is there sufficient storage space and are pupils instructed to bring food to the department for it to be stored at the correct temperature?

Equipment and resources/class sizes

This covers a wide range of equipment, from storage through to large and small equipment.

In terms of food storage, is there sufficient capacity for pupils to store ingredients at the correct temperature? If not, do you/do pupils limit ingredients to those that do not need special storage? Is there space for the cooked products to be chilled and stored before collection at the end of the day?

Does the food teaching room have sufficient cookers and other equipment to allow all pupils to cook? If not, how do you manage this?; if classes are split, how can you ensure that those not engaged in practical work are doing something worthwhile? Some possible solutions to this include:

- group work, with groups of pupils sharing 'sets' of equipment;
- pupils cooking different products so that different types of equipment is required;
- rotating the work, with pupils undertaking a variety of activities – this can be difficult to supervise and needs to be carefully planned.

Does the school have any industry-standard equipment? Many schools have not yet been able to afford equipment of this kind, but consider what might be possible: electronic scales, temperature probes, bread-making machines. Other ways in which pupils could emulate industrial practice include ensuring the correct setting for all machines and equipment used, monitoring times and temperatures and using quality assurance procedures.

There are many ways in which ICT can be used in food technology, this is discussed in more detail in *Learning to Teach Design and Technology in the Secondary School* (Owen-Jackson 2007).

Lesson times

In many schools, lessons last for between 50–70 minutes, this is a very short period of time for pupils to arrive, prepare themselves and their food, learning points to be made and the room to be cleared and prepared for the next group. Again, it raises questions about the decisions of what to cook. Some teachers try to alleviate the problem by asking pupils to prepare ingredients at home, for example, rubbing in fat and flour for the first stage of making pastry, but this can mitigate the learning experience; others ask technicians to pre-weigh ingredients but this also denies pupils the opportunities to develop these skills.

Food dishes also need to be thoroughly cooked, part-cooked food should not be sent home. Again, though, leaving food in the oven for you or the technician to take out means that pupils miss out on a valuable learning experience so consideration needs to be given to what can be achieved in the time available – this will vary according to the age and ability of the pupils.

And how, with all this, do you find time to include starter activities, learning points in the lesson and evaluation of products? This can partly be achieved through careful planning over a sequence of lessons so that, over a period of time, pupils experience a wide range of activities. Effective teaching will also guide pupils to see how these experiences link together and how what they learnt in one lesson, or another area of Design and Technology, can be transferred to another lesson. The Ofsted report on food technology in secondary schools (Ofsted 2006) gives some examples of good practice.

Activity 3.4   Planning for effective teaching

Download the Ofsted report from the website: www.ofsted.gov.uk. Either type 'HMI 2633' in the search box or go to 'publications', select the letter 'F', and find the report. Read through the report and note what is identified as good practice. Are there elements of this in your teaching or are there ideas in the report that you could incorporate into your teaching to make it more effective?

The report identifies that effective teaching in food technology enables pupils to undertake a wide range of practical activities; this includes practical work to develop theoretical understanding, such as experimentation and investigation, and to design and develop product ideas. The context in which work is set often offers opportunities to develop subject knowledge, for example, through making nutritional aspects a constraint or requiring the use of specific ingredients or manufacturing processes.

FOOD TECHNOLOGY AND THE WIDER SCHOOL CURRICULUM

In addition to contributing to pupils' learning across the curriculum (see Chapter 9) food technology contributes to the 'Healthy Schools' initiative (see www.wiredforhealth.gov.uk and www.foodinschools.org) and Every Child Matters agenda (see www.everychildmatters. gov.uk). Both these initiatives are concerned with the physical health and well-being of pupils, with food and nutrition playing an important part. In some schools there appears to be a tension between teaching food technology as part of Design and Technology and teaching pupils about nutrition and practical cooking skills. This, I argue, is a false dichotomy – pupils need to understand about nutrition, and the nutritional needs of groups within the community, in order to undertake food product development. They also need to develop their practical skills in order to make their food products. Food technology does not have to focus on biscuits, pizzas and cakes because these lend themselves to short lessons and industrial practice, pupils could engage in developing savoury biscuits, sauces, soups and other healthy products to develop knowledge and skills that meet National Curriculum food technology requirements and that develop their nutritional knowledge and practical skills.

SUMMARY

This chapter has briefly considered what is taught in food technology and made recommendations for you to audit and monitor your own subject knowledge. It has discussed the role of 'designing' within food and suggested that you review the food product development activities that pupils in your school undertake. Constraints on the teaching of food technology have been considered, and although this has raised more questions than answers, it is hoped that it will have enabled you to consider provision in your own school and how you can make best use of this. The development of the wider contribution that food technology can make to the school curriculum was also introduced, this is an area in which you will need to keep yourself updated.

REFERENCES

Bielby, G. (2005) 'Teachers' experiences of teaching young people about the food industry', in E. Norman, D. Spendlove and P. Grover (eds) *DATA International Research Conference 2005*, Wellesbourne: DATA

DATA (2003) *Minimum Competences for Trainees to Teach Design and Technology in Secondary Schools*, Research Paper 4, Wellesbourne: DATA

DfEE/QCA (1999) *Design and Technology: The National Curriculum for England*, London: HMSO. www.nc.uk.net

DfES (2004) *Key Stage 3 National Strategy Foundation Subjects: Design and Technology Framework and Training Materials*, London: HMSO

Ofsted (2006) *Food Technology in Secondary Schools*, London: Ofsted. www.ofsted.gov.uk report ref. no. HMI 2633

Owen-Jackson, G. (2000) *Learning to Teach Design and Technology in the Secondary School*, London: Routledge

Owen-Jackson, G. (ed.) (2001) *Food Technology: Developing Subject Knowledge in Design and Technology*, Stoke on Trent: Trentham Books/The Open University

Rutland, M., Barlex, D. and Jepson, M. (2005) 'Designing in food technology – a curriculum intervention strategy in a one year design & technology postgraduate teacher training course', in E. Norman, D. Spendlove and P. Grover (eds) *DATA International Research Conference 2005*, Wellesbourne: DATA

FURTHER READING

Proudlove, R.K. (2001) *The Science and Technology of Foods*, London: Forbes

Shaw, R. (ed.) (1996) *Product Development Guide for the Food Industry*, Chipping Camden: Campden and Chorleywood Food Research Association

WEBSITES

All the major food companies have websites, many of which contain useful information for teachers.

www.foodforum.org.uk
This site provides information on food technology issues and resources for use in the classroom.

www.foodinschools.org
This Department of Health/Department for Education and Skills provides information on the Food in Schools programme.

www.nutrition.org.uk
This is the website of the British Nutrition Foundation and provides information on nutrition, as well as details of resources and conferences.

Chapter 4   Materials technology in the classroom

NIGEL ZANKER

INTRODUCTION

The aim of this chapter is to guide you through strategies which enable you to apply your knowledge and skills to your teaching of materials technology (in some schools this may still be referred to as 'resistant materials'). As a materials technology specialist you may be expected to be able to teach pupils aged 11–18 to design and make products primarily using wood, metals and plastics; if this is your second area of expertise, you will be expected to teach it to pupils aged 11–14.

Applying your expertise to teach pupils to design and make is an enjoyable and rewarding task. It is also a daunting one, especially if you have not sufficiently planned and prepared the lesson! The latter is important; you must design and make your own examples of the projects you set for pupils as this will give you insight into the difficulties that pupils may face and provide ideas about opportunities to extend projects. It will also give you confidence and raise your 'street-cred' because it shows pupils that you actually know what you are doing.

By the end of this chapter you should be able to:

- apply your subject knowledge of materials technology to your teaching;
- identify opportunities for development in your subject knowledge;
- understand how schemes of work meet statutory requirements;
- have considered how to encourage pupils to develop their designing skills;
- use resources from curriculum development initiatives in your teaching.

SUBJECT KNOWLEDGE FOR MATERIALS TECHNOLOGY

Materials technology involves mainly working with wood, metals and plastics, but you should also make use of other materials such as ceramics and modelling materials like card and foams. You will make use of ICT for Computer Aided Design and Manufacture (CAD/CAM) as well as for generic applications such as word processing, spreadsheets, databases and web-based research. In schools, work in materials technology usually incorporates elements of structures, mechanisms and sometimes electronics (see Chapter 2); developing your own subject knowledge so that you can cover this range will help you to undertake diverse and exciting projects.

During your training you undoubtedly will have acquired new skills and knowledge, even if this is your specialist area, and the development and application of subject knowledge in the classroom will be an ongoing process. It is important that you feel confident in your subject knowledge and skills when teaching projects as lack of expertise on your part would result in ineffective teaching, and pupils would make poor progress. Remember, from this chapter's introduction, the importance of pupils knowing that you can do what you say!

Activity 4.1 introduces you to the competences expected of newly qualified teachers specialising in materials technology (Design and Technology Association 2003).

Activity 4.1 Materials technology subject knowledge audit

Below are the competences required for those with materials technology as their first specialist area. Complete the grid using two different coloured highlighters to indicate your strengths and areas to be developed.

	1 Designing: Newly qualified teachers should be able to:	
1	Accurately sketch construction details, using, where appropriate, recognised conventions that show how a wide range of materials might be used to make artefacts.	
2	Accurately draw construction details using formal drawing techniques, to show how wood, metal and plastics can be used to make artefacts.	
3	Use more complex models to test a technological principle.	
4	Use fundamental computer solid modelling to manufacture from 3D toolpaths.	
5	Create complex assemblies of computer-generated solid models to confirm the accurate interaction of separate components.	
6	Create 3D computer-rendered images that clearly show the desired surface qualities.	
7	Generate detailed working drawings using CAD, including assembly, parts and sectional views.	
8	Access design data, using IT relating to, for example, the properties of materials, standard sizes, fixings, adhesives and components.	
9	Undertake spreadsheet analysis for costing and simulation of batch production.	
10	Investigate, disassemble and evaluate a range of products made from resistant materials, including modern and smart materials.	
11	Analyse and investigate advanced manufacturing industrial technologies used to make mass-produced consumer products.	
12	Analyse and investigate the visual and other sensory principles when analysing artefacts.	
13	Recognise the importance of new technologies, innovations and inventions in the design of consumer products.	
14	Consider a range of products and evaluate their impact on the environment.	
15	Analyse the social consequences of automated mass-production systems.	
16	Consider how the psychological aspects of ergonomics can influence the design of products.	
	2 Making: Newly qualified teachers should be able to:	
1	Use the properties and working characteristics of a range of resistant materials including smart materials.	
2	Accurately measure and mark out considering appropriate tolerances when using both precision hand tools and machines, during the manipulation of a wide range of resistant materials.	
3	Accurately cut and waste, by using machines, wood, metal, plastics to efficiently achieve precision fit and quality finish.	

Activity 4.1 *continued*

4	Accurately deform, form and fabricate a range of materials, using appropriate methods, by using complex equipment and machine tools.	
5	Effectively join a range of materials using advanced techniques, complex equipment and appropriate machinery.	
6	Use CAD/CAM to aid manufacturing to achieve appropriate and repeatable quality, reliable function and ensuring fit.	
7	Consider visual and other sensory principles when using materials to meet design requirements.	
8	Recognise that systems and control can be integrated with a range of materials to design and make artefacts.	
3	**Knowledge and Understanding: Newly qualified teachers should be able to:**	
1	Consider and analyse the physical, chemical and working properties of a wide range of woods, metals and plastics (including modern and smart materials), and how the arrangement of particles and fibres in the material influence its properties.	
2	Understand how materials can be combined and processed to create useful properties.	
3	Understand how the structure of wood, metal and plastics influences use and effectiveness.	
4	Understand how materials are combined together in a structural way to resist forces.	
5	Understand how wood, metal and plastics resist forces, such as compression, tension, torque and bending.	
6	Understand how a wide range of standardised components influence manufactured products.	

Source: Adapted, with permission, from the Design and Technology Association (2003).

This will have given you some indication of how well prepared you are to teach materials technology, and may have indicated some areas that you need to develop. What is important, though, is what you will be required to teach in your own school. Activity 4.2 will help you to think about this; in order to do the task, you will need to obtain copies of the schemes of work that you will be teaching.

Activity 4.2 Analysing schemes of work

Looking at the schemes of work that you will be teaching and following the guidance on mind-mapping in Chapter 2 of *Learning to Teach Design and Technology in the Secondary School* (Owen-Jackson 2007), use the diagram shown in Figure 4.1 to identify the knowledge and skills required to teach these projects.

A blank version of Figure 4.1 is given on the following page copy this and complete it so that you have one for each scheme of work and for each record the tools, materials and processes to be used. Then use two different coloured highlighter pens: one to identify those tools, materials and processes with which you are competent and the other for those that you need to develop.

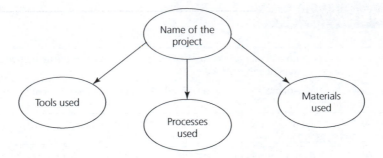

Figure 4.1 Analysing projects in materials technology

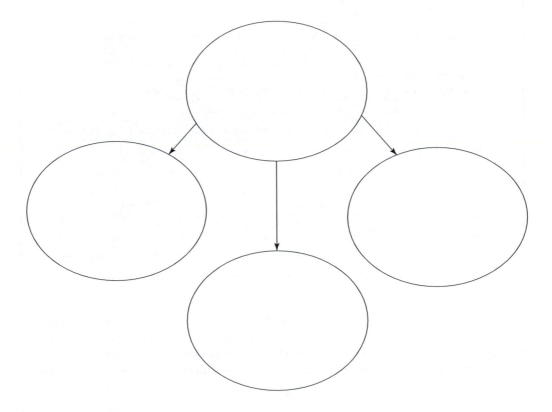

Activity 4.3 Preparing to teach materials technology

Now, for each analysis of a scheme of work that you have undertaken, complete the questions on the following page.

DEVELOPING PUPILS' DESIGNING SKILLS

Designing is considered to be the least well-taught aspect of Design and Technology (DfES 2004) and there have been several initiatives to improve this. The Key Stage 3 National Strategy materials for Design and Technology contain many useful suggestions for activities to help pupils develop their design skills, see Module 4 in DfES (2004). Other design

Activity 4.3 *continued*

Do you have the required subject knowledge and skills, if not, how will you develop these?
What knowledge and skills will the pupils learn? Are these clearly articulated?
Where might pupils experience difficulties? Are you prepared to respond to these?
What resources are required? Are these available, if not, how do you obtain them?
Throughout Key Stage 3, do pupils' knowledge and skills build progressively, increasingly becoming more complex and challenging?
Are pupils given opportunities to develop wider skills, e.g. literacy and numeracy?
Do pupils have opportunities to work with ICT within the materials technology context?
Are economic, social, moral and cultural issues addressed? Are environmental and sustainable issues addressed?
Over the course of Key Stage 3, each of the above points should be answered positively; if not, are there any ways in which the schemes of work could be amended? Does this review raise any issues about your own professional development? Are there areas where you need to further develop your professional knowledge? If so, you may need to talk to your head of department or a senior member of staff.

strategies, some of which will help you develop your own skills in this area, can be found in Owen-Jackson (2001). Giving pupils 'stories' of how products they know were invented can also stimulate them, information can be found in Harrison (2004) and van Dulken (2002) or try putting 'inventions' into a search engine.

However, in materials technology, designing does not always take place with pencil and paper. Design ideas can be generated and developed from pupils 'playing around' with materials and finding out what they can do. This strategy was used by a school where pupils were asked to design a new lightshade; they were given the wire frame and a range of resources and used this as the basis of their design work (see DATA 2005).

There are also several software CAD packages used in schools, for example, ProDesktop, TechSoft and SolidWorks (www.prodesktop.net www.techsoft.co.uk or www.solidworks. com). Find out which design software is used in your school and, if you are not already familiar with it, spend some time learning how it works.

CURRICULUM DEVELOPMENTS IN MATERIALS TECHNOLOGY

Schools' schemes of work are written to meet the requirements of the National Curriculum for Design and Technology (DFEE/QCA 1999) or for awarding body examination specifications (syllabuses). The National Curriculum and examination specifications outline the subject knowledge and skills to be taught but do not specify projects, these are left to the creativity and imagination of the teacher. Resources to support teachers in developing suitable schemes of work for Key Stage 3 are available from the DfES/QCA (1999). The Key Stage 3 National Strategy for Design and Technology (DfES 2004) also offers materials to help teachers plan for effective teaching and learning. These resources can be downloaded from the Internet (see Further Reading for web addresses). However, it is unlikely that you will be able to simply download these and use them as they are. They will provide a good starting point and give you ideas for what can be done, but you will need to adapt the resources to meet the needs of your own school and its pupils.

There are also commercial publications available to help with the development of schemes of work for Key Stages 3 and 4. Look to see what is currently in your school or obtain copies from the publishers. Again, you will need to assess whether or not they suit your circumstances. Questions to ask about each resource include:

- Do I have the resources to be able to teach this? Consider materials, equipment, time and your own knowledge and skills.
- Is the scheme clear? Are the learning outcomes articulated? Are these the learning outcomes that I want for my pupils?
- Will the scheme interest and motivate the pupils I teach?

You might also want to ask whether or not the scheme addresses the cross-curricular issues and themes such as sustainability, or whether it incorporates the use of ICT. Before selecting a commercial resource, you need to consider what you want the pupils to learn and whether or not the scheme will enable this. If not, think about whether you could adapt it or whether it is just unsuitable for this school, these pupils or this particular learning outcome.

Materials technology is an area that continues to develop as new materials and new processes are introduced, for example, polymorph is increasingly being used in schools, as are thermocolour sheets, metal paper and phosphorescent sheet. You will need to keep up to date with these, as well as with new initiatives such as education for sustainable development. Ways to do this are to visit websites (some useful ones are given in Further Reading at the end of this chapter), attend conferences and meetings and talk to teachers.

SUMMARY

In the introduction to this chapter, we outlined the breadth and depth of subject requirements expected of you as a materials technology teacher. The activities in the chapter are designed

---

Activity 4.4 Making use of curriculum developments

For each project that you are, or will be, teaching make a copy of the table below. Summarise each project and attach photographs to provide a visual record of your own progress in developing your subject knowledge.

Activity 4.4 *continued*

Project title	Year group

Educational benefits to pupils in designing and making this project:
How does this build on pupils' existing skills and knowledge? What new knowledge and skills will they learn?

Curriculum links
For example, National Curriculum programme of study, examination specification, DfES/QCA schemes of work, National Strategy for Design and Technology.

Resources available
For example, National Strategy worksheets, curriculum development initiative materials, IT resources.

Teaching strategies used

New knowledge and skills I have developed	Photographs to illustrate my development

to help you apply your existing skills and knowledge and to enhance these through curriculum developments in teaching. The development of your designing and making skills will be a never-ending process, and continued personal development is essential for innovative teaching.

Finally, remember that you are not alone. You have been encouraged in this chapter to discuss with teachers, and discussion is a two-way process. As an aspiring new teacher you have skills and knowledge that are more recent but, as yet, you are inexperienced at how to deliver them. This is why it is important that you analyse strengths and opportunities for development using schemes of work in your school. There is, therefore, a synergy arising from imparting this knowledge and learning how it can be taught. The rewards are personal satisfaction and motivated pupils.

REFERENCES

DATA (2005) 'Industry and creativity', *DATA Practice*, 6: 2–4

Design and Technology Association (2003) *Minimum Competences for Trainees to Teach Design and Technology in Secondary Schools*, Wellesbourne: DATA (www.data.org.uk)

DfEE/QCA (1999) *Design and Technology: The National Curriculum*, London: QCA

DfES (2004) *Design and Technology: Framework and Training Materials Key Stage 3 National Strategy, Module 4: Teaching the Subskills of Designing*, www.standards.dfes.gov.uk/keystage3/respub/design/training4/

DfES/QCA (1999) *Design and Technology Schemes of Work for Key Stage 3*, www.standards.dfes.gov.uk/schemes2/

Harrison, I. (2004) *The Book of Inventions*. London: Cassell.

Owen-Jackson, G. (2000) *Learning to Teach Design and Technology in the Secondary School*, London: Routledge

Owen-Jackson, G. (ed.) (2001) *Developing, Planning and Communicating Ideas: Developing Subject Knowledge in Design and Technology*. Stoke on Trent: Trentham Books/The Open University

Van Dulken, S. (2002) *Inventing the 20th Century: 100 Inventions That Shaped the World*. London: The British Library

FURTHER READING

Denton, H. (2000) 'Teaching resistant materials', in G. Owen-Jackson (ed.) *Learning to Teach Design and Technology in the Secondary School*, London: RoutledgeFalmer

Eggleston, J. (2001) *Teaching Design and Technology*, 3rd edn, Buckingham: Open University Press

WEBSITES

www.curriculumonline.gov.uk
This website provides information on resources that can be purchased by schools using e-learning credits.

www.data.org.uk

www.stepin.org
Run by Practical Action, this site provides information, resources and case studies for teaching about sustainability.

www.tep.org.uk
The Technology Enhancement Programme website provides information and resources on many aspects of teaching materials technology.

Chapter 5

Textiles technology in the classroom

ALISON WINSON AND SUE WOOD-GRIFFITHS

INTRODUCTION

Textiles technology, as with all areas of the Design and Technology curriculum, continually develops as materials and equipment develop, ICT applications expand and new technologies become more affordable. You are referred to *Learning to Teach Design and Technology in the Secondary School* (Owen-Jackson 2007) for details of the subject knowledge audit and we recommend that you also look at the updated 'minimum competences' recommended for textiles technology teachers (DATA 2003). In this chapter we consider how textiles technology is taught in the classroom.

By the end of this chapter you should:

- understand how to develop projects that ensure pupils make progress, and how to involve pupils in assessing their own progress;
- have considered ways of encouraging the development of pupils' design skills;
- have considered some of the social, cultural, environmental and economic issues in textiles technology;
- have considered ways of using ICT to teach textiles;
- know how to organise and manage the physical teaching space and equipment in a textiles classroom.

DEVELOPING TEXTILES PROJECTS

How can you ensure that pupils make progress in the development of their knowledge, skills and understanding of textiles technology? First, you will need to find out what they have already done and consider how you can develop their existing skills as well as introducing new skills, knowledge and understanding. For pupils in Year 7, finding out what they have covered in their primary schools is essential. Your school may have a Key Stage 2/3 co-ordinator who could help or you may need to contact teachers in feeder schools. Asking Year 7 pupils to bring in items made at primary school and allowing some 'show and tell' time can help in assessing their capabilities.

Second, you will need to consider how to differentiate the work so that individual pupils can make progress, whatever their starting point. One way to do this is to plan a project in which the product can be simplified or made more challenging according to the abilities of the pupils, for example, hats, bags, book covers and mobile phone cases. *Learning to Teach Design and Technology in the Secondary School* (Owen-Jackson 2007) discusses differentiation in greater depth.

Consider, also, the time available. Pupil progress is hampered, and pupils become frustrated and disinterested, if there is insufficient time to complete the work. You may need to seek guidance initially but knowing what is 'do-able' will come with experience.

Activity 5.1 Progression in pupils' learning in Key Stage 3

To have a better understanding of the progression of skills, knowledge and understanding across Key Stage 3, complete the table below using the schemes of work from your school.

	Year 7	Year 8	Year 9
Textile Project			
Skills taught			
Knowledge and Understanding			

Now answer the following questions:

Is there clear progression of skills, knowledge and understanding across the key stage? How do you know?

Could there be better progression of skills, knowledge and understanding? If so, how could this be achieved?

Involving pupils in reflecting on their progress

Monitoring pupil progress in textiles can be challenging for a student or newly qualified teacher but there are strategies you can use that will help, and that will involve the pupils in reflecting on their own progress. Pupils can be asked to keep 'diaries' in which they record their progress and set themselves targets. This allows you to see what they have done and how they are making progress, as well as requiring pupils to take some responsibility for their learning. Some pupils also find it motivating, especially if those who achieve their targets are rewarded according to the school's rewards policy.

One student teacher introduced target setting in lessons by asking pupils to note down at the end of a lesson what they intended to have done by the end of the following lesson. Then, at the end of the following lesson she asked them to look back at their targets and to note whether or not they had attained their target, and if not, the reason why this was so.

Self-assessment is usually conducted at the end of a design and make activity, with pupils asked to write an evaluation. These evaluations are often of poor quality because pupils have not been taught how to evaluate. To help them improve you can provide a 'writing frame' as shown in Figure 5.1. Alternatively, you could model for them how to structure an evaluation by talking them through what you would do if you were to asked to do it.

The product I have made is

It is intended to

It does this well because

It could be improved if I

Market research on my product indicates

Figure 5.1 Evaluation writing frame

Peer assessment can also help pupils to develop their evaluative skills. This can be done by asking pupils to display their work around the room with 'PostIt' notes attached. Ask them to look carefully at each other's work and write two positive comments and one area for development or improvement. You may have to model this before pupils embark on the activity by demonstrating how you would do it and explaining the comments that would be appropriate; word banks can help with this and will help to develop subject-specific vocabulary. If your school has the necessary ICT equipment, peer assessment can be done using electronic voting cards, with pupils voting for or rating other pupils' work. This way of working has the advantage of anonymity and may encourage pupils to be more honest.

Displays of pupils' work in the classroom can have many positive effects on learning. First, pupils are able to consider the work of a previous group before embarking on their own project. Undertaking peer assessment of the displayed work could be a good starting point. Second, pupils gain a great deal of pride and satisfaction from seeing their work displayed. Finally, good quality work displayed in prominent areas, for example, in a reception area, can enhance the profile of the subject among pupils, staff and parents.

DESIGNING IN TEXTILES TECHNOLOGY

As with the other focus areas, pupils can find the design work in textiles difficult so you need to find ways to encourage them. The section on using ICT (see below) suggests using a slide show of images or a moodboard as an inspiration for design ideas. There are also software programs that will aid design work, for example, PaintshopPro or ArtCam. SpeedStep is a textiles-specific program designed to help pupils create initial sketches of textiles products, including garments, and to design styles, patterns and logos for printing.

Design inspiration can also be taken from the work of a particular designer, era or movement, for example, ask pupils to use Art Deco or punk styling to produce a design for a product. In the Key Stage 3 National Strategy Design and Technology materials (DfES 2004), there are several activities suggested to help pupils generate and develop ideas, many of which could be used in textiles technology.

SOCIAL, CULTURAL, MORAL AND ECONOMIC ISSUES

If pupils are to 'become discriminating and informed users of products, and become innovators' (DfEE 1999/QCA, p. 15) then awareness of the social, moral, environmental and cultural issues associated with the textiles industry are important aspects of pupils' learning. Social and moral issues can be raised in discussion of fair trade issues, with pupils investigating where their own clothing and footwear are manufactured and considering the implications of this, and through the consideration of the environmental consequences of textile work, such as the production of synthetic materials and dyes. The Sustainable Technology Education Project (STEP) (www.stepin.org) is a useful classroom resource.

Social and economic issues can be raised through encouraging pupils to use recycled materials and components in their work. Limiting them to only using recycled materials can be challenging and creative, and contribute to the development of their designing and making skills. At Key Stage 4, case studies can be used to illustrate sustainability, for example, the 'Recycled Fleeces' case study on the STEP website.

Cultural and historical influences on design can easily be addressed in textiles lessons; visual aids and classroom displays can be developed from old fashion items and textiles from around the world. Using focused tasks pupils can examine the dyeing and construction techniques on these samples and consider the different influences on fabric products in this country, for example, batik, embroidery, mola and shisha techniques. They can then practise these techniques in a series of focused practical tasks before making decisions about what to use in their own work.

Discussing 'fair trade' issues with pupils often involves the economics of trade, so you may need to do some research in this area, and the website of Practical Action (www.practicalaction.org) may help.

Economic issues also arise when teaching about manufacturing, discussing how manu-facturers keep down costs, reduce waste and improve profits. You can raise pupils' awareness of economic issues by how you deal with resources in the classroom, for example, ensuring that fabric is used in a cost-effective way. You can also be innovative, for example, designing projects around materials that are easily obtained, such as one school did when using curtain fabric offcuts and lining provided free by a local curtain manufacturer. Fleece fabric is a recycled material and presents a cheap alternative to using felt, and buying fleece blankets or throws from mill shops and market stalls can be cheaper than purchasing fabric by the metre. Fleece can be used successfully for making toys, mascots and hats and in quilting projects.

Activity 5.2   Sustainable issues

Look at the 'Sustainable Technology Education Project' website www.stepin.org. Using one of the case studies from the site, e.g. 'organic cotton to fair trade fash-ion', and using the pro-forma provided by your school or training provider, plan a lesson to raise pupils' awareness of the sustainability issues associated with the textiles industry.

Smart materials

Pupils need to have an understanding of the modern textiles industry and modern and 'smart' materials, such as reflective strips in outdoor clothing, thermo chromic dyes, micro fibre fabrics and polar fleece.

Pupils' understanding of the use of 'smart' materials can be developed through product evaluation, practical investigation or incorporating their use into a design brief. A search for 'smart' textiles using your favourite search engine will lead you to many websites that provide technical information and describe many innovative uses of smart materials in the textiles industry (see Further Reading for details of websites).

Activity 5.3   Smart materials

Start a collection of products that demonstrate the use of smart materials, e.g. reflective jackets or bags, moisturising tights, thermo sensitive t-shirts, moisture-sensitive nappies. Using the pro-forma provided by your school or training provider, plan a lesson to introduce pupils to smart materials and incorporate a product evaluation task.

ICT IN TEXTILES TECHNOLOGY

The use of information and communications technology (ICT) continues to grow rapidly and is transforming the way that pupils learn and teachers teach. *Learning to Teach Design and Technology in the Secondary School* (Owen-Jackson 2007) discusses in depth how to become familiar with the ICT policy and facilities in school and suggests ways of incorporating general computer applications such as databases, the Internet and design packages into lessons. Here we consider how you could use ICT to enhance the teaching of textiles tech-nology and how it could help pupils develop their creativity, enhance the presentation of their work and model industrial practices.

Expansion in the use of interactive whiteboards and data projectors has enabled teachers to unleash their own creativity to inspire and motivate pupils with interactive, creative and purposeful resources. For example, a search engine such as Google or a dedicated website such as Flickr will allow you to download images (remember to check copyright) that you can load into a slideshow on PowerPoint to flood the pupils' imaginations with ideas to inspire their own designing.

Construction processes, for example, using 'bondaweb' for appliqué, can be modelled and digitally photographed. The photographs can then be put into a PowerPoint slideshow and looped throughout the lesson for pupils to refer to as necessary. Alternatively they could be printed onto cards and used for a card sort or line-up activity to engage pupils in thinking the process through. These techniques also encourage pupils' independent learning and contribute to differentiated lessons.

When teaching industrial practices, computerised sewing machines offer scope for pupils to develop an understanding of consistency and quality control procedures as well as illustrating CAD and CAM.

The digital camera has great potential in the classroom for pupils to record their work, including mistakes, for portfolios or to present using PowerPoint. Encouraging pupils to use a digital camera and a computer to produce a storyboard of their progress can support the development of their understanding of a process. It can also assist in the assessment process as you can question pupils about their decisions retrospectively using their photographs as a basis for discussion.

Here are some suggestions for ways in which you could use ICT to produce resources for the classroom; they could be done by you or pupils:

- Choose a design theme and use a search engine, e.g. Google images, to collect images and put them into a slide show as inspiration for design ideas.
- 'Crop' some of the images and paste them together to produce a moodboard to use for design inspiration.
- Use a digital camera to produce a step-by-step account of a simple process, such as threading the sewing machine, or a construction technique, e.g. inserting a zip. Put the images into a PowerPoint presentation. How else could you use these images within the classroom?

MANAGING THE TEXTILES TECHNOLOGY CLASSROOM

The practical nature of textiles technology means that you have to consider carefully how to manage the resources within it in order to help pupils' learning. Here we identify some important aspects for you to consider:

- The layout of the room, the positioning of work tables and equipment are important – if possible, have pupils seated facing you as this will ensure they can see and hear you when you are speaking. There should then be an area of the classroom suitable for you to carry out demonstrations, where a group can fit comfortably and easily see what you are doing. There will also need to be a dedicated area, with access to a sink, for messy or wet activities such as painting and dyeing.
- The positioning of equipment needs careful thought to ensure a safe environment, for example, wax pots need to be away from the main work area, sewing machines, irons and ironing boards near to be close to sockets to avoid trailing electrical leads. Tabletop ironing boards can be safer and ease space restrictions in a crowded classroom.
- It is essential that small equipment, such as pins, needles and scissors, is monitored; counting equipment out at the start of a lesson and back in at the end is good practice. Having sets of equipment, for example, scissors, pins, thread, tape measures, etc., which can quickly be given out can aid this and equipment sets can be easily checked by you or a pupil at the end of the lesson. Alternatively, needles can be attached to

individual pieces of paper on which pupils write their names; this also gives increased responsibility to pupils.

- One example of a way in which you could make clearing away more efficient is with the use of 'tidy up cards'. Decide what activities are required in order to clear the room at the end of the lesson and put each one of these activities onto a card, for example, 'collect in the scissors' or 'pick up all the bits from the floor'. Give out cards to pupils once they begin to clear away. This will work better with classes in Key Stage 3 but for older pupils you could try, for example, flashing the 'tidy up' activities onto the board using PowerPoint; perhaps even adding a timer!

- Well-maintained equipment helps to ensure the smooth running of lessons, for example, sewing machines should be checked regularly to ensure tensions are correctly set and needles sharp, scissors should be sharpened. A technician, if available, may be able to service machines, wind bobbins, change machine needles, mix dyes, sharpen scissors and cut fabric but check with the Head of Department before asking for this work to be done.

- If the department orders and stores fabric for pupils to purchase, you will need to find out how the school manages this, and how fabric is made available to pupils, for example, do they have a free choice or is choice limited in some way? How do they pay, will you be responsible for collecting money? If so, how is this recorded and stored?

A well-managed classroom helps to promote pupil learning and contributes to a purposeful learning environment, it will be important for you to quickly establish control of your classroom.

SUMMARY

This chapter has considered some of the practical implications and considerations for teaching textiles technology effectively. You have been encouraged to think about how to manage the classroom to ensure pupils make progress and have a variety of experiences during Key Stage 3; you have also been asked to consider how some of the ideas can be developed and presented at Key Stage 4. As you gain experience you will build on these to create your own ideas for developing pupils' Design and Technology capability.

REFERENCES

DATA (2003) *Minimum Competences for Trainees to Teach Design and Technology in Secondary Schools*, Research Paper 4. Wellesbourne: DATA

DfEE/QCA (1999) *The National Curriculum for England: Design and Technology*, London: HMSO

DfES (2004) *Key Stage 3 National Strategy Foundation Subjects: Design and Technology Framework and Training Materials*, London: HMSO

Owen-Jackson, G. (2000) *Learning to Teach Design and Technology in the Secondary School*, London: Routledge

WEBSITES

www.data.org.uk
www.practicalaction.org
www.stepin.org
www.nano.org.uk/textiles
www.osnf.com
www.smartextiles.co.uk

These websites provide information on smart and modern materials.

www.antiapathy.org/wornagain
www.suitcase-london.com
www.tinglondon.com
www.traid.org.uk

These websites provide information on sustainable textiles.

Chapter 6   Design and technology and vocational education

TIM LEWIS

INTRODUCTION

This chapter discusses vocational education which is being introduced into schools in an effort to tackle the shortage of skills within the English workforce. These new provisions will present teachers and schools with exciting new opportunities. A key aspect of vocational courses is the work-related element, which attempts to introduce the knowledge, understanding and skills required for specific areas of employment; in Design and Technology these relate to the food industry, manufacturing, engineering and hospitality and catering. As a Design and Technology teacher it is likely that you have specific subject knowledge and understanding which are relevant to the implementation of vocational diplomas in schools.

While Design and Technology can make a contribution to vocational education, there are also issues which will need to be discussed and resolved in schools during the planning process and initial phase of implementation. It is likely you will find this topic is being discussed in your school's staff room and it will be helpful to you to join in this debate.

By the end of this chapter you will:

- know about the relationship between vocational education and Design and Technology;
- have an understanding of the vocational examination specifications;
- have explored some of the teaching and learning support materials available;
- appreciate how your knowledge and expertise can be used within vocational education.

DESIGN AND TECHNOLOGY AND VOCATIONAL EDUCATION

The history of Design and Technology, and the subjects which preceded it, is littered with references to the vocational aspects of the subject; woodwork, metalwork, technical drawing, domestic science and needlework were directly linked to employment opportunities or, for girls, work in the home. Later curriculum developments focused on GCSE and National Curriculum, while in further education they began to develop the General National Vocation Qualification (GNVQ) system which found its way into the Key Stage 4 curriculum. These early GNVQ courses were then followed by the development of vocational GCSEs (see below).

Following a review of GCE A-levels, which became known as the 'Tomlinson Report', the government published the document *14 to 19: Opportunity and excellence* (DfES 2003) which introduced the 14–19 Diploma scheme. These vocational diplomas are to be offered in parallel with traditional A-level courses.

The 14–19 Diploma Scheme

A range of diplomas has been proposed and Design and Technology is strongly aligned to several, shown in bold in Table 6.1. Others provide opportunities for Design and Technology involvement; these are shown in italics in Table 6.1. It is important to recognise that a diploma is not a specific subject but a 'learning line' and so while Design and Technology teachers can contribute to the teaching of a course, it is unlikely that they will be able to do it all.

Table 6.1 14–19 Diploma, proposed lines of learning

Phase	Diploma area	Available from
Phase 1	1. *ICT* 2. *Health and Social care* 3. **Engineering** 4. Creative and Media 5. *Construction and the Built Environment*	September 2008
Phase 2	6. Land-based and Environment 7. **Manufacturing** 8. Hair and Beauty 9. Business Administration and Finance 10. *Hospitality and Catering*	September 2009
Phase 3	11. Public Services 12. Sport and Leisure 13. Retail 14. *Travel and Tourism*	September 2010

So what is the structure of a diploma course likely to be? At the time of writing, the details of the Diplomas are still being planned but guidelines issued by the Qualifications and Curriculum Authority (QCA) indicate that there will be three levels:

Level 1 Diploma

- provides learners with Foundation learning, in particular in generic skills;
- main learning programme with 240 guided learning hours*;
- learners to explore opportunities for progression within at least one line of learning;
- fits alongside and, where appropriate, supports National Curriculum study pre-16.

Level 2 Diploma

- provides opportunity for substantial learning in relation to a particular main line of learning – 450 guided learning hours*;
- co-exists with and, where appropriate, supports National Curriculum study;
- where appropriate, provides opportunities for learners to be ready for employment or to progress to work-based learning.

Level 3 Diploma

- level 3 could be delivered as a two-year full-time programme;
- main learning programme – 600 guided learning hours*
- extended project 180 guided learning hours*.

Note: *Guided learning hours (GLHs) are those for teaching, set tasks and projects.

It is interesting to note the inclusion of generic skills; these include 'soft skills', functional mathematics, literacy and ICT. Functional mathematics and literacy place these subjects into 'real-world' situations and are being developed in schools. Soft skills include communication skills, teamwork, problem-solving, negotiating and leadership, which are easily taught through Design and Technology work.

The guidelines are clear that diplomas will be taught mainly in schools with work experience as a key feature of each level. The target is that, by 2013, 40 per cent of 14–19-year-olds will be studying a vocational diploma and these will account for half of their curriculum time in school.

Interested organisations are developing outline specifications. Not surprisingly, the Science, Engineering and Manufacturing Technologies Alliance (SEMTA) is developing Engineering and has established the Engineering Diploma Development Partnership (EDDP). Scrutiny of the planning (www.engineeringdiploma.com) shows that the diploma will give young people an understanding of three key elements of engineering: people, processes and systems, with learning outcomes divided into the following key themes:

Level 1

The engineered world, discovering engineering and engineering for the future.

Level 2

Introduction to the world of engineering, technology (maths and science), technology (engineering), design principles, computer aided engineering (CAE), produce an engineered system or product, electronic and electrical systems, quality control and maintenance.

Level 3

Health and safety, business improvement, technology (maths and science), design principles for computer aided engineering (CAE), materials technology, innovative design enterprise, contracting and tendering, organisational behaviour, process control systems and maintenance planning.

Work experience is integrated into the learning and can be sector-specific to enable schools to work with local industry. For example, schools in the vicinity of an aerospace industry could tailor the learning to meet the needs of this industry; alternatively, schools can adopt a more general approach and work with several smaller enterprise industries.

Many of the proposed themes for Engineering are already present in Design and Technology teaching, with the exception of human factors and business. The challenge for many schools will be finding ways in which to work in a more integrated way with maths and science.

In parallel with the development of the diploma is the introduction of a vocational specialism for schools. These schools will celebrate and champion vocational innovation and excellence. By January 2006, there were 46 such schools and the target for 2008 is 200 vocational specialist schools.

Activity 6.1   Finding out about vocational education

Explore the Specialist Schools and Academies Trust Vocational Specialism website http://www.ssatrust.org.uk/vocationallearning/default.aspa. Follow the links to <curriculum development> and <case studies>. Read the case studies and try to identify any similar initiatives in your school. These could be school initiatives and not necessarily based in the Design and Technology department. Note below any school-based developments and how you might become involved in these.

From the Specialist Schools and Academies Trust Vocational Specialism website http://www.ssatrust.org.uk/vocationallearning/default.aspa. and Activity 6.1 note any school-based developments and how you might become involved in these.

If your school has links with a College of Further Education, explore what is available for pupils in the 14–16 age range. Make notes here.

In my opinion, vocational education is concerned with offering pupils an integrated learning experience; it should not be about specific subjects having a vocational label. So, while Design and Technology can make a valuable contribution to vocational education, it should not be considered a vocational subject. Given this approach, Design and Technology teachers may be able to lead some vocational courses and make a unique contribution to others.

VOCATIONAL GCSE EXAMINATIONS

In 2002, eight GCSE courses in vocational subjects were introduced to the school curriculum, these were:

- Applied art and design
- Applied business
- Engineering
- Health and social care
- Applied information and communication technology (ICT)
- Leisure and tourism
- Manufacturing
- Applied science.

Subsequently, Performing arts and Construction and built environment were added. These courses are designed to capture the interest shown by many Key Stage 4 pupils in linking their school-based education to work. A key feature is that they advance pupils' knowledge, understanding and capability in specific vocational areas. They also develop 'soft skills' which, in the GCSE courses, include:

- management of resources;
- interpersonal skills;
- information handling;
- understanding systems;
- knowing how to use technology;
- literacy;
- numeracy;
- thinking skills;
- personal qualities: responsibility and self-management.

The courses encourage practical and work-related learning and are designed to have the same rigour and standards as other GCSE subjects. They are designated 'double award' courses, making them the equivalent of, and requiring the same curriculum time as, two GCSEs.

While none of the vocational GCSEs bear the title 'Design and Technology', some are closely related, for example, Engineering has a strong materials technology element; Manufacturing is concerned with the manufacture of goods in a range of industries. There is considerable application of Design and Technology principles and practice in the Construction and built environment course and food technology teachers can make a contribution to Health and social care and Hospitality and catering. Opportunities also exist for Design and Technology to contribute to ICT and Applied science courses. To gain a greater understanding of how Design and Technology can contribute to vocational GCSEs, scrutiny of the specifications is a useful exercise; Activity 6.2 asks you to do this.

Activity 6.2 Vocational GCSE

Go to one or more of the following award board websites and search for 'vocational GCSE'. Read through relevant specifications and think about the contribution that you could make to such a course. On the following page note your thoughts about the specification and where you consider you could make a contribution.

OCR	http://www.ocr.org.uk/OCR/WebSite/docroot/index.jsp
AQA	http://www.aqa.org.uk/qual/appliedgcse.html
Edexcel	http://www.edexcel.org.uk/home/

TIM LEWIS

Activity 6.2 *continued*

From the award board websites note your thoughts about the relevant GCSE vocational specification you research and where you consider you could make a contribution.

Since their introduction, the vocational GCSEs appear to have been successful. In 2004, Ofsted reported that pupil achievement is 'satisfactory or better in three quarters of lessons' and achievement 'is often good in engineering'. The courses are also reported to improve the behaviour of pupils.

In introducing vocational courses, some schools have experienced organisational difficulties, particularly where a contribution is required from several departments. Some schools also report problems with the need to integrate industrial practice into the courses. The integration of industrial practice raises two issues for Design and Technology. First, in current Design and Technology work, the focus has been on pupils' individual design and make work with the 'outcome' being a priority. This may need to be reviewed as much industrial practice involves team work and experimentation. Second, although many teachers have good links with a number of businesses and companies, preparation of pupils for work placements is often minimal and so pupils cannot capitalise on the opportunities available. This issue would need to be addressed for pupils to gain greater benefits. Two schools have already successfully addressed these issues, as discussed in the following two case studies.

Case Study 1

Broxtowe College (http://www.broxtowe.ac.uk/) is a Centre of Excellence for Vocational Education (CoVE) (http://www.lsc.gov.uk/National/Partners/CoVEsand NSA/default.htm) and has developed an innovative range of BTEC courses in association with East Midlands airport. The College has a realistic mock-up of an airline cabin used for training cabin crew and this has enabled them to offer short work experience courses for Key Stage 4 pupils doing GCSE Tourism and Leisure Management.

Case Study 2

The Group Training Centre (GTA) Doncaster (http://www.doncastergta.co.uk/) is an advanced training centre for the motor vehicle trades. In the minds of many teachers, parents and pupils this conjures up the 'oily rag' image but this 'high-tech' centre provides training for basic tyre and exhaust fitter level through to Advanced City and Guilds and Institute of Motor Industry management qualifications. They also provide week-long courses for pupils in the 14–19 age range designed to meet the needs of vocational courses in schools. These courses include classroom teaching and practical tasks using electronic simulators as well as vehicles provided by the franchise dealers. As the Centre negotiates with the school what is required, the courses can contribute to Engineering or Applied business GCSE.

Activity 6.3 Vocational qualifications

Explore the range of vocational qualifications available and look at case studies on the Qualifications and Curriculum Authority (QCA) 14–19 Learning website http://www.qca.org.uk

To see how vocational education is presented to pupils, explore the Vocational Learning website http://www.vocationallearning.org.uk/students

TEACHING AND LEARNING SUPPORT MATERIALS

A range of resources is being developed to support teachers who are required to teach these new vocationally-based courses, visit the Learning and Skills Network website (http://www.vocationallearning.org.uk/teachers/) which has information for teachers, parents, students and employers. For teachers, the site provides, in addition to operational information, a wealth of teaching and learning material from schemes of work to downloadable assignments. Particularly impressive is the support for teachers' planning for work placements. The Learning and Skills Network also extends to regional and local groups of teachers developing and promoting good practice in this rapidly developing aspect of the 14–19 curriculum. Activity 6.4 asks you to explore this network in your region.

Activity 6.4 Learning and Skills Network

Find out more about the Learning and Skills Network group in your area. Access this through http://www.vocationallearning.org.uk/regions/. Select your region from the Route Summary menu, then select your county. You will find the name and address of the local contact. For each entry there are downloadable Network Output files. Have a look at several of these and consider what they could contribute to your teaching. Note any relevant points below.

From the Learning and Skills Network website http://www.vocationallearning.org.uk/regions/, note here any relevant points.

SUBJECT KNOWLEDGE TO TEACH VOCATIONAL EDUCATION

Many Design and Technology teachers have industrial or business experience and this fits them well for Diploma teaching. However, it will be necessary for those contributing to the teaching of the Diplomas to have an up-to-date knowledge of current practice in the relevant vocational area. For example, food technology teachers will need an understanding of current practice in the food production industry and/or catering in hotels. Additionally, it will be essential for teachers to regularly refresh their industrial and business knowledge. It will be important to develop links with industry and business, not only to benefit pupils but also to provide teachers with opportunities for work-based learning and professional development. It is also likely that the award boards will provide training in their own specifications.

In addition to subject knowledge, teachers will have to consider their pedagogical knowledge and practice as vocational courses require the development of a *work-related curriculum* – this is not the same as providing *work experience* for pupils. The challenge will be to find ways of integrating an understanding of industrial or business practice into your teaching. This aspect is still emerging and requirements are not yet finalised, but you will need to consider *how* you teach these courses as well as what you teach.

The Design and Technology Association/Nuffield publication (2005) *Creativity in Crisis* sets out some concerns about the National Curriculum for Design and Technology and the constraints of the examinations; and there is the suggestion that over-regulation has impeded innovation within the subject. However, Design and Technology is a popular subject in schools, with considerable growth at A-level, and the emerging Diploma structure puts Design and Technology teachers in a strong position to re-establish themselves as curriculum innovators. However, we must accept that we cannot do it all, we will need to liaise with teachers of mathematics and science. Linking learning in schools with work placements is a major challenge. And, of course, there is the initial hurdle of explaining Diplomas to parents and pupils in an education system which has focused on the National Curriculum and GCSE examinations.

SUMMARY

After several attempts to get vocational education into schools it seems that a determined effort is being made to develop vocational diploma courses for the 14 to 19 age range. The diplomas are to be phased in to schools over a three-year period from 2008. A key change is that they are not subjects but 'learning lines' with several subjects making a contribution, and the inclusion of 'soft skills' to make pupils more employable is an important feature.

Vocational GCSE examinations have been established in many schools, with Design and Technology making a significant contribution to the teaching. These examinations pave the way for the emerging diplomas. There is a well-developed national and regional support network available, offering support in establishing links with business and industry. The Specialist Schools and Academies Trust has identified vocational education as a specialism, with high performing schools adopting this as an additional specialism.

Many newly qualified and established Design and Technology teachers are well equipped to contribute to vocational education and the emerging diplomas provide exciting new opportunities and challenges. Kimbell and Perry (2001) sum up Design and Technology's position relative to vocational education: 'Design and Technology is in the vanguard of those preparing youngsters for employment in the knowledge economy.' The development of vocational diplomas within our education system once again provides an opportunity to be innovative and lead the way.

REFERENCES

DATA/Nuffield (2005) *Creativity in Crisis: Design and Technology at KS3 and KS4*, Research Paper 18, Wellesbourne: DATA

DfES (2002) *14–19: Curriculum and Qualifications Reform*, DfES 0976–2004, London: HMSO

DfES (2003) *14–19: Opportunity and Excellence*, DfES 0744/2002, London: HMSO

Kimbell, R. and Perry, D. (2001) *Design and Technology in the Knowledge Economy*, London: Engineering Council

Ofsted (2004) *Developing New Vocational Pathways: Final Report on the Introduction of New GCSEs*, OfSTED Publications Centre Document HMI 2051, London: Ofsted

FURTHER READING

British Vocational Qualifications, 7th edn, (2004) London: Kogan Page

Chapman, C. and Whitehouse, G. (2000) *Intermediate GNVQ Engineering* Harlow: Pearson Education

Cushing, S. (2004a) *GCSE Engineering*, London: Hodder and Stoughton

Cushing S. (2004b) *GCSE Manufacturing*, London: Hodder and Stoughton

Donaldson, S., Gray, A. and Padayache, R. (2003) *GCSE Leisure and Tourism (Double Award)*, London: Hodder Education

Pring, R. (1986) *The Curriculum and the New Vocationalism*, The Stanley Lecture, Royal Society of Arts, Sheffield

Standish, A. (2001) *The Key to Skills*, Spiked Culture. http://www.spiked-online.com/Articles/00000000548D.htm

Yeomans, D. (1996) *Constructing Vocational Education: From TVEI to GNVQ*, University of Leeds School of Education Occasional Publications series. http://www.leeds.ac.uk/educol/documents/00002214.htm

WEBSITES

www.aqa.org.uk
www.edexcel.org.uk
www.ocr.org.uk
The above three awarding bodies all offer vocational examination courses, their websites give specifications for these courses.

www.broxtowe.ac.uk/
This is the website for Broxtowe College, one of the case studies referred to in the chapter.

www.dfes.gov.uk/14–19/index.cfm?sid=1
This website, run by the Department for Education and Skills, provides information on 14–19 opportunities.

www.doncastergta.co.uk/
This site gives details of courses run by Doncaster Motor Trades.

www.engineeringdiploma.com
This is the SEMTA Engineering Diploma website.

www.lsc.gov.uk/National/Partners/CoVEsandNSA/default.htm
Run by the Learning Skills Council, this site provides information on Centres of Vocational Excellence and National Skills Academies.

www.semta.org.uk/semta.nsf/?Open
The Science, Engineering, Manufacturing Technologies Alliance provides information and guidance on education and careers in those areas.

www.thetridenttrust.org.uk/default.asp
This site provides information on work experience and work-related learning.

www.vocationallearning.org.uk/teachers/
Run by the Learning Skills Network, this site contains detailed information about vocational curriculum, work-related learning and relevant courses.

Part 2 Teaching Design and Technology

Chapter 7 Teaching and learning in Design and Technology

GWYNETH OWEN-JACKSON

INTRODUCTION

It has been acknowledged that 'the quality of teaching is a key factor in determining the quality of pupils' learning and the standards they achieve' (Ofsted/DfEE 1995, p. 13). This chapter will help you to understand more about pupils' learning and what you can do to improve the quality of your own teaching.

By the end of this chapter you should:

- be aware of the range of learning styles that pupils may use;
- understand that there are different influences on pupils' ability to learn;
- have considered how to encourage pupils' creativity;
- have considered how to encourage independent learning;
- be aware of a range of teaching strategies that you can use.

FACTORS AFFECTING PUPILS' LEARNING

There is a body of research on how pupils learn and some of this has influenced school teaching. Learning theories present ideas about how children learn, with implications for how they should be taught. The main learning theories are behaviourism, constructivism and social constructivism; these are discussed in detail in *Learning to Teach in the Secondary School* (Capel *et al.* 2004). Understanding these learning theories will help you to better understand what is happening in the classroom and so be able to respond to this.

Learning styles, in contrast, refer to individual pupils' approaches to learning and these have been classified in a number of different ways. Table 7.1 presents some of the suggested classifications.

You will see that there is some overlap in these classifications and that they address similar ideas. The V-A-K learning styles are promoted in the Secondary National Strategy (DfES 2003), so these are the ones most likely to be discussed in your school. This categorisation, as have others, has been criticised and you should not believe that this is the only tool to inform your planning for individual needs. These categorisations, even if accurate, only define pupils' *preferred* approach and you should encourage pupils to use different approaches in order to develop a wide range of skills. Activity 7.1 will help you to think about how to use a variety of approaches in your teaching.

Table 7.1 Learning styles

Learning style	Description, pupils learn:
Honey and Mumford (1983)	
Activists	by doing
Reflectors	through feelings and experiences, especially observing
Theorists	through observation and investigation
Pragmatists	by thinking things through and experimenting
Kolb (1984)	
Divergent	from feelings and personal experience
Assimilator	from experience, uses this to inform abstract thinking and understanding
Convergent	from abstract reflection
Accommodator	from concrete and active experience
Gregorc (1986)	
Concrete sequential	using concrete or tangible props, when information is presented sequentially in small steps and they can follow instructions
Concrete random	using concrete or tangible props and open-ended tasks in which they can 'play around' with possible solutions
Abstract sequential	by exploring ideas and concepts in their mind; they are logical and linear thinkers and prefer their work to be structured
Abstract random	through thinking and reflecting, they prefer to be personally involved in their learning and for it to have personal relevance to them
Bishop and Denley (1997)	
Dynamic learners	through action and involvement
Common sense learners	through organisation and instructions, usually independent
Imaginative learners	by using their imagination and thinking things through, they like group work
Analytical learners	through analysis and logic, they are usually well organised and prefer to be independent
V-A-K	
Visual learners	through information presented visually
Auditory learners	through listening to information
Kinaesthetic learners	through being physically involved with their learning

---

Activity 7.1 Learning styles

In the following table, identify and note as many different ways of teaching that you can think of, using specific Design and Technology examples. Some examples have been provided for you. When you are planning lessons, use this worksheet to help you consider which strategies to use and to broaden your range of teaching strategies.

Activity 7.1 *continued*

Learning style	Description	Possible teaching strategies
Honey and Mumford (1983)		
Activists	by doing	
Reflectors	through feelings and experiences, especially observing	
Theorists	through observation and investigation by	Experimental work with materials
Pragmatists	thinking things through and experimenting	
Kolb (1984)		
Divergent	from feelings and personal experience from	A visit to a manufacturing company to consider work-planning
Assimilator	experience, uses this to inform abstract thinking and understanding	
Convergent	from abstract reflection	
Accommodator	from concrete and active experience	
Gregorc (1986)		
Concrete sequential	using concrete or tangible props, when information is presented sequentially in small steps and they can follow instructions.	
Concrete random	using concrete or tangible props and open-ended tasks in which they can 'play around' with possible solutions.	Product analysis as a starting point for design work
Abstract sequential	by exploring ideas and concepts in their mind; they are logical and linear thinkers and prefer their work to be structured.	
Abstract random	through thinking and reflecting, they prefer to be personally involved in their learning and for it to have personal relevance to them.	
Bishop and Denley (1997)		
Dynamic learners	through action and involvement	
Common sense learners	through organisation and instructions, usually independent	
Imaginative learners	by using their imagination and think things through, they like group work	Through role play to develop client specifications
Analytical learners	through analysis and logic, they are usually well organised and prefer to be independent	

The theory of multiple intelligences, suggested by Gardner (1993) has also been used to explain ways in which pupils learn, although the theory was not specifically developed for education. Multiple intelligences describe different strengths that pupils bring to the classroom, these are said to be:

- linguistic
- logical-mathematical
- musical
- visual-spatial
- bodily-kinaesthetic

- intrapersonal
- interpersonal
- naturalist
- spiritual.

Pupils will realise their potential in these areas if they have the opportunities to do so. In your teaching, therefore, try to present pupils with a range of tasks and activities to develop different skills and abilities. This is relatively easy to achieve in Design and Technology as we work with words, pictures, products, use practical skills, work individually and in groups and consider values.

Influences on pupils' learning

There are, of course, many other influences on pupils' learning, including:

- physical differences and gender;
- intellectual abilities;
- emotional state;
- social background;
- cultural background.

In Design and Technology gender differences become more apparent when pupils select their examination subject; the majority of boys choose materials technology or ECT and the majority of girls choose food or textiles technology. And in Design and Technology, as in most other subjects, girls attain higher grades in tests and examinations. There are ways in which you can address these gender differences. Research conducted in the late 1970s (SEAC 1991) identified that boys performed better in 'active' tasks, while girls favoured 'reflective' ones, and that boys preferred 'industrial' contexts, while girls preferred those connected to people. The research also found that although boys preferred tasks to be well defined they worked better when their work time was less structured, for girls, the opposite was true. While this is a complex area, influenced by curriculum, teaching and assessment as well as expectations and pre-conceptions, at this stage you need to be aware of these differences and ensure that, over a period of time, you plan to meet the different abilities, capabilities, preferences and interests of boys and girls in order to help both achieve their potential in the subject.

In the same way, while you have little control over the intellectual, emotional, social and cultural backgrounds of pupils, you should be aware of them and, as far as possible, take account of them when planning your teaching.

CREATIVITY

There is still debate over what is meant by 'creativity' but here it is taken to mean two things:

- creative teaching – using a range of interesting teaching strategies to engage and motivate pupils;
- creativity in pupils – work produced by pupils that is imaginative and innovative, at the pupils' level.

Creative teaching

The key to creative teaching is to use a wide range of strategies so that pupils do not become used to one way of doing things. Some possible ways of being creative include:

- ensuring your classroom provides a stimulating and creative environment, through the displays and artefacts it contains;

59

- keeping up to date with new developments in materials and processes and introducing these to pupils where possible;
- using contemporary culture as a context for pupils' work, for example, films, television programmes, news items, the latest 'craze';
- using a range of teaching strategies;
- use competitions, awards and challenges in your teaching;
- keeping up to date with Design and Technology news through reading professional magazines and websites, as these can often give you new ideas for classroom activities and new ways in which to teach.

Creativity in pupils

A number of factors influence pupils' capacity for being creative, some inherent such as personal qualities, and some external. Designing is the aspect of Design and Technology most closely associated with creativity, as we ask pupils to generate and develop ideas for products; this aspect is also the least well taught (DfES 2004). Creativity can also be demonstrated through the way in which pupils approach and solve problems, the way in which they apply knowledge to the development of products and the way in which they work with materials. Your role as a teacher is to provide opportunities for pupils to be creative, present them with strategies for developing their creativity and to support them as they practise their skills. Providing a supportive environment in which pupils feel safe to take risks and make mistakes is a good starting point for developing creativity, and this will come about through developing good relationships and modelling and supporting risk-taking and failure. Although it is acknowledged that in the current target- and standards-driven climate this may be difficult to do in your school, you could try with just one class or year group to find out what impact it has on pupils' work.

The Secondary National Strategy materials for Design and Technology (DfES 2002) contain many useful ideas for activities to encourage pupils' creativity. You will need to select activities appropriate to your topic and your pupils, and you may need to adapt what is presented, but you will find a wealth of ideas in the pack. Look at the pack (which should be in your school) to help you with Activity 7.2.

Activity 7.2   Creativity

Think of one lesson that you will be teaching next week, if this is not possible, use a lesson that you have previously taught. From what you have read, observed in school and drawn from the Secondary National Strategy materials, consider how you could make your teaching more creative and/or develop pupils' creativity in the lesson. Make notes on strategies you could use, then write or amend your lesson plan to incorporate these.

Make notes here on ways in which you could make your teaching more creative and/or develop pupils' creativity in the lesson.

PERSONALISED LEARNING

I have already referred to some of the individual needs that pupils have, and which you should plan for. *Learning to Teach Design and Technology in the Secondary School* (Owen-Jackson 2007) discusses differentiation in more detail and considers the needs of pupils with Individual Education Plans/Programmes (IEPs).

'Personalised learning' is now being promoted by the government as a way of raising standards. Personalised learning refers to making learning appropriate for pupils' individual needs, interests and aptitudes. In order to do this you will need to consider individual needs, as discussed above, use assessment data (see Chapter 11) to find out pupils' achievements and targets and use a range of teaching strategies. Design and Technology is well placed to develop personalised learning because of the individual nature of many of the design and make activities and because of the range of teaching strategies employed.

Personalised learning also involves the wider school in that it means providing pupils with the most suitable curriculum, which may involve diplomas (see Chapter 6) or out-of-school learning.

DEVELOPING INDEPENDENT LEARNING

In secondary education we tend to guide pupils in their learning, setting out what they will learn, the order in which they will learn it and what they will do to learn it. This is not helpful to pupils when they leave school, whether for higher education or work, where they will be expected to demonstrate the ability to work independently. Some pupils will be able to make this leap but many will need support and guidance to develop the necessary skills; we can begin to foster these skills throughout pupils' secondary education.

There is a range of skills that demonstrate independent learning (see DfES 2003), these include:

- being well organised and able to prioritise tasks;
- able to use a range of strategies to solve problems, including asking for help when necessary;
- able to gather information using a range of resources, and able to sift and select information;
- being an effective team member, able to take on different roles if necessary;
- able to put together ideas and concepts to create 'the bigger picture' in their own thinking;
- able to self-assess and set their own targets and actions.

Design and Technology can contribute to the development of these independent learning skills, but work will need to be carefully planned to ensure that it happens. For example, pupils can be asked to:

- plan their own work schedule, graduating from being given headings by you to planning using flow charts to planning their own project;
- use a range of problem-solving techniques;
- use a range of information-gathering and selecting techniques, moving from using resources provided by you to resources suggested by you and supplemented by their own to eventually being able to select and use their own;
- work in groups, first of all guided by you in the roles that they will take and moving on to developing their own teams;
- self-assess their own work, provided with templates initially and guided by you, moving through to developing their own assessment criteria and undertaking realistic self-assessments of their own work.

Other strategies that help to promote independent learning include:

- sharing learning objectives and outcomes with pupils;
- discussing assessment criteria with pupils;
- encouraging higher-order thinking (see Chapter 9).

Activity 7.3 Independent learning

Primary pupils often experience a higher level of independence in their learning than do secondary pupils. Look at a Year 7 scheme of work that you are, or will be, involved in teaching and note in the table opposite where it currently allows for independent learning. If possible, amend the scheme, using some of the suggestions above, to promote the skills of independent learning.

TEACHING STRATEGIES

Understanding pupils' needs is only one side of the equation, you also need to be able to use a range of teaching strategies in order to meet those needs. *Learning to Teach Design and Technology in the Secondary School* (Owen-Jackson 2007) discusses when and how to teach using exposition, questioning, demonstration, group work, project work and ICT. The strategies of modelling and out-of-school learning are discussed below.

Activity 7.4 Teaching strategies

One way of expanding your range of teaching strategies is to observe other teachers at work. Arrange to observe a number of different teachers in your school, both within Design and Technology and in other departments. On p. 64, note the teaching strategies they use, the contexts in which different strategies are used and any interesting features. Later, try to incorporate these strategies into your own teaching.

Modelling

In Design and Technology, modelling usually refers to the technique whereby pupils create a 2D or 3D model of the product they are designing or intend to make. Here it has a different meaning; modelling as a teaching strategy refers to your ability to demonstrate to pupils what you want them to do. We frequently use demonstrations as a form of modelling, showing pupils how to carry out a practical task, but modelling can be used for other processes. For example, through 'thinking aloud', you could model for pupils how to conduct a product analysis; through writing up on the board as you work through it, you could model how you would evaluate or plan your work.

Modelling through 'thinking aloud' allows pupils to follow the process so remember to include the questions that you would ask yourself, and why, the uncertainties that you might experience and how you would record your outcomes. You might then sum up what you had learnt from the product analysis and how this would inform the next stage of your work.

Year 7 Scheme of Work	
Topic:	
Current scheme	Amendments to promote independent learning
Aims:	
Objectives:	
Content:	
Teaching strategies:	
Pupil activities:	
Assessments:	

Activity 7.4 *continued*

Teaching strategies used	Context (year group, topic)	Interesting features

After modelling a process, you could then work through an example with pupils before asking them to carry out the process independently. Similarly, with a written plan of work, you could either work through an example with them or provide an example; discussing what you had to consider and how you constructed your plan, using the format that you want pupils to use. When designing, where pupils often want sketches to look neat and tidy, you could model how you design, talking as you fill a page with annotated sketches of ideas and showing what you expect of them.

Out-of-school learning

Out-of-school learning, such as visits to industrial premises or shopping areas, fieldwork to conduct surveys, observations or consumer questioning, can help to make learning real and interesting for pupils. However, as with any teaching strategy, you must consider whether or not it will help pupils attain the planned learning objectives and outcomes, no teaching is effective unless it does this.

Having decided that an out-of-school activity is appropriate, you must then ensure you follow the correct procedures for planning and conducting such activities. Your school should have a designated Education Visits Co-ordinator and before undertaking any out-of-school activities, make sure that you contact this person to discuss policy and procedures.

Activity 7.5 Out-of-school learning

Out-of-school activities, such as visits to industrial premises, can be very interesting for pupils studying Design and Technology. You should always liaise with your school's Education Visits Co-ordinator when arranging out-of-school learning. Use the checklist below when organising out-of-school activities.

Tick when done	Procedures checklist
	Speak to the Education Visits Co-ordinator and ensure you know and understand school policies and procedures
	Plan what needs to be done to follow the school policies and procedures: who needs to be contacted, and when; who needs to be informed and when; what consents need to be gained; what special arrangements need to be made
	Visit the 'site' in advance, liaise with personnel there to ensure that the purpose of the visit is known and understood
	Agree, in writing, the roles and responsibilities of those involved in the visit
	Prepare pupils for the visit, discuss with them its purpose and learning objectives
	Make sure any worksheets, question sheets or record sheets are prepared. Book any audio-visual recording equipment you may need
	Give pupils, in writing, details of arrangements for the day – consider dress codes, meeting places and times, lunch arrangements and any equipment they will need
	After the visit – discuss with pupils what was learned, whether learning objectives were achieved and where this fits into their work
	After the visit – thank the external contacts and, if appropriate, provide them with feedback
List below any school-specific requirements:	

Using your voice

It is worth noting here that whatever teaching strategy you select you are likely to be using your voice to communicate to pupils, so you need to think about the best ways in which to do this. *Learning to Teach in the Secondary School* (Capel *et al.* 2004) discusses the use of voice in detail and you are recommended to read this.

SUMMARY

This chapter has presented a lot of information about pupil learning and suggested various teaching strategies for you to consider. It may seem like a lot to think about when you are learning to teach but, as with learning to drive, if you focus on each of the discrete actions in turn, you will soon be able to put them together to be an effective teacher in the classroom.

REFERENCES

Bishop, K. and Denley, P. (1997) *Effective Learning in Science*, Stafford: Network Educational Press

Capel, S., Leask, M. and Turner, T. (2004) *Learning to Teach in the Secondary School: A Companion to School Experience*, London: Routledge

DfES (2002) *Key Stage 3 National Strategy Foundation Subjects: Design and Technology*, London: DfES

DfES (2003) *Teaching and Learning in Secondary Schools: Pilot*, London: DfES

DfES (2004) *Key Stage 3 National Strategy Foundation Subjects: Design and Technology Framework and Training Materials*, London: DfES

Gardner, H. (1993) *Frames of Mind: The Theory of Multiple Intelligences*, London: Fontana

Gregorc, A. (1986) *Adult's Guide to Style*, Gregorc Associates

Honey, P. and Mumford, A. (1983) *Using Your Learning Styles*, Peter Honey Publications

Kolb, D.A. (1984) *Experiential Learning: Experience as a Source of Learning and Development*, Englewood Cliffs, NJ: Prentice-Hall

Ofsted/DfEE (1995) *Design and Technology Characteristics of Good Practice in Secondary Schools*, London: HMSO

Owen-Jackson, G. (2000) *Learning to Teach Design and Technology in the Secondary School*, London: Routledge

SEAC (1991) *The Assessment of Performance in Design and Technology*, London: SEAC

FURTHER READING

Gardner, H. (1999) *Intelligence Reframed: Multiple Intelligences for the 21st Century*, New York: Basic Books

WEBSITES

www.data.org.uk

www.ncaction.org.uk/creativity
The National Curriculum in Action website is run by the Qualifications and Curriculum Authority and provides 'practical ideas on how to promote pupils' creative thinking and behaviour'.

www.youngforesight.org
The Young Foresight project was designed to encourage Year 9 pupils to be more creative in their design thinking. This website provides details of the project and some of the outcomes.

Chapter 8 Using ICT in Design and Technology

GWYNETH OWEN-JACKSON

INTRODUCTION

The role of ICT in schools has grown rapidly, and continues to do so. There are two aspects to its role; that of enhancing pupils' learning in Design and Technology and that of making your administrative work easier. This chapter considers teachers' use of ICT for their own work, although this is connected to work in the classroom. Pupils' use of ICT is considered in *Learning to Teach Design and Technology in the Secondary School* (Owen-Jackson 2007).

One of the difficulties about writing about ICT is how quickly text goes out of date as new technology is adopted and what is available in schools varies. The availability of ICT hardware and software in the Design and Technology department depends to some extent on the budget and the disposition of the school and department; some spend large sums of money and have interested, innovative staff, some don't have either of these and some have one but not the other! So, this chapter describes some of the technology currently found in most schools and ways in which you can use it in your teaching of Design and Technology. It also describes some emerging technologies that may be available now in some schools and, it is hoped, will soon spread to all schools.

By the end of this chapter you should be aware of:

* the potential of ICT to enhance your teaching;
* the role of ICT in teachers' administrative work;
* emerging technologies and their potential for use in Design and Technology.

TEACHERS' USE OF ICT

ICT can be used by teachers for a number of activities including keeping your own subject knowledge up to date, planning and conducting lessons, assessment and record keeping, so you need to become familiar with the tools for these activities. Using ICT can ease your workload if you use it to work more efficiently or effectively, for example, word-processed lesson plans are easily amended and updated and spreadsheets make analysis of pupil data quicker and easier. There are some generic applications of ICT that you will be able to use and some school-specific information management systems that you will need to find out about in your own school and become familiar with.

ICT and teaching

When planning lessons, as mentioned above, you can use word-processing or desktop publishing packages so that your plans can quickly and easily be amended and updated.

You can also share electronic plans with other teachers both within your department and across wider communities.

To help you with the content of your lesson plans there are hundreds, if not thousands, of web-based resources to draw on. Some websites offer you teacher-prepared resources that you can adapt, and if you have some good ideas yourself, you might consider uploading your own work to these sites, they include: www.teachernet.gov.uk, http://contentsearch. becta.org.uk, www.tes.co.uk/resources and www.data.org.uk. Other websites provide you with ideas that you can draw on, for example, www.qca.org.uk and www.ncaction.gov.uk. And others contain subject-specific content that you can integrate into lessons, such as www.dtonline.org.uk and www.data.org.uk. There are also hundreds of general websites that may have relevance for particular projects, for example, the British Museum, the Design Museum, the BBC, or individual company websites. Many more web links can be found using a search engine such as Google, Yahoo! or AskJeeves. You could also try putting 'search engines' into Google or your favourite search engine to discover others!

Activity 8.1 Beginning to explore

It is best if you use a computer with broadband access for this task, either at home or in your school. You will also need to set aside at least an hour, more if you have the time.

Look at each of the websites given above – at this stage there is no need for you to do anything or write anything down, just spend some time browsing and becoming familiar with what is available. You might, of course, find something that you will be able to use in your classroom straight away!

The range of ICT available to make teaching more interesting and effective is growing fast. I outline below some of the hardware and software that you may find in your school and consider how you might use it to enhance your teaching.

You will probably be familiar with *interactive whiteboards*, also known as electronic boards or smart boards. Although the underlying principles are the same, each board operates in a slightly different way so you will need to become familiar with the board in your own department or classroom. Training is usually available from the provider of the board and there is guidance available on the web, try www.thereviewproject.org.

Once you have prepared resources for the board, you will be able to save them, use them with different classes and update them when necessary. Interactive whiteboards have been criticised, see www.becta.org.uk/research, for making pupils passive 'consumers' of information but when properly used, they can making learning more effective so you need to plan your use of the whiteboard carefully.

You will probably also know that *data projectors* and *computers* can be used in a similar way to electronic whiteboards, but without the interactive element. You can use a data projector and computer to show PowerPoint presentations, scanned documents and photographs and links to websites. This allows you to prepare lessons in advance, store them electronically, amend and update them quickly and easily and share them with colleagues. You can even link them to your electronic calendar so that they are easy to find on the day that you need them – store the file on your computer, open your Outlook Calendar and select the date and time of the lesson, insert the details, click on 'attachment' (paper clip icon) and add the file to your calendar, remember to 'save and close'. When you go to the lesson this could save valuable minutes of searching for the file you spent ages creating.

Viewers are a useful piece of equipment to use in Design and Technology, alongside the data projector. Viewers allow you to transmit through the projector large-scale images of whatever is on the viewer, and one school uses them in Design and Technology to show pupils how to do soldering as all the pupils can clearly see what is happening, which is not the case when they are trying to peer over your shoulder!

PowerPoint presentations can be used in a number of ways. Most simply you can use a series of slides to illustrate your exposition, explanation or demonstration. A short PowerPoint presentation quiz could be presented as a timed slideshow and used as a starter activity while you are registering pupils. You could also use a series of photographs to demonstrate how to carry out a particular task, for example, threading up a sewing machine, using a food processor or pillar drill. The photographs could then make up a series of slides which would cycle through so that pupils could watch the demonstration again or focus in on parts they were unsure about; this would also support the development of pupils' independent learning.

PowerPoint slides can be made more interesting with the insertion of audio or video clips. This can be done using the 'Insert' – 'Movies and Sounds' menu in PowerPoint; this also allows you to record your own sound so you could put in a 'voice over' on demonstration slides.

There is another feature that allows you to insert boxes into slides for pupils to make choices or insert text. Go to 'View' menu – select Toolbars – select 'Control Toolbox'. In the Control Toolbox the first icon inserts a tick box, allowing pupils to make multiple choices, for example, from a given list they could select all the equipment or processes they had used to make a product. The second icon inserts a text box into the slide, allowing pupils to write to a PowerPoint slide, and this could be used to personalise a presentation. The third icon inserts an option box, this allows pupils to select one option from a range of possible answers and could be used in a quiz-type format.

Activity 8.2   PowerPoint resources

For this task you will need access to a computer with PowerPoint software. Think of a lesson that you will teach, or have taught, and in which you could use a PowerPoint presentation; this could be one that includes a demonstration or group work, or simply an explanation.

If you are a beginner with PowerPoint, then put together a series of slides to cover the basic information from the lesson. This could be slides with a series of questions or statements, it could be instructions for pupils to follow. The software will help you do this if you use the PowerPoint Wizard. When you have prepared the slides, play around with them – try changing the background, the colours and the fonts or adding animations; these will all be found on the menu buttons.

If you have used PowerPoint before, then consider ways in which you could improve your skills, for example, can you add photographs, audio clips or option boxes as described above?

If possible, use the PowerPoint presentation in a lesson and evaluate how effective it was.

Both electronic whiteboards and data projectors allow you to make links to websites, which can make your teaching more dynamic. There are hundreds of possible websites available and you will need to research in advance to find suitable ones. It is also advisable to keep a record of websites. You could do this by adding them to your 'Favourites' or you could use a social bookmarking site, such as www.del.icio.us. This allows you to store and access your favourite websites, use tags to describe them, and makes them accessible for sharing with others. You could keep a notebook, use ICT tools such as a word-processed document, spreadsheet or database, or use your social bookmarking tags, to note which websites relate to which scheme of work, or lesson, and some comment about the content. Finally, if you only periodically visit a website, remember to check it before the lesson as sites can, and do, change.

Almost all schools now have networked systems and broadband connections (99 per cent according to teachernet.gov.uk). These allow you to store lesson plans and other information on school systems so that they are instantly accessible in the classroom, to you and to pupils and other teachers if you wish. In some areas Regional Broadband Consortia have been established as centres to promote good practice and provide advice and guidance, find out if there is a consortium near you by accessing http://broadband.ngfl.gov.uk/

Other generic items that may be available include digital cameras and video equipment. Digital cameras can be used to record pupils' progress in designing and/or making. Some Award Boards require photographs to be attached to examination coursework and digital cameras make this much easier and quicker – and safer, it has been known for film sent for processing to be lost or damaged! Digital photographs could also be used for a number of classroom activities, for example:

- in sorting and classifying activities, these could be computer-based or printed photographs;
- in determining client/user needs, again computer-based or printed photographs can be used to illustrate 'scenarios' to pupils;
- as research material;
- as learning aids for pupils with learning difficulties or those with English as an additional language.

Video equipment can be used to record pupils' progress, or to record a number of activities, for example, client/user groups or industrial processes.

There is also subject-specific ICT equipment that you need to be familiar with, such as computer-controlled machinery in materials technology, computerised sewing and embroidery machines, food industry equipment used in schools such as conveyor ovens. Again, availability varies from school to school so you will need to find out what is used in your school and practise to ensure you become confident in using it.

You are likely to have had some experience of subject-specific software, such as ProDesktop or SpeedStep, but find out what is used in your school. Some schools use ArtCam, SolidWorks or other CAD programs and there are a number of nutritional analysis programs used. I recommend that you spend time learning how to use these programs so that you can incorporate them effectively into lessons. However, remember that there are likely to be some pupils who are much more proficient with the software than you are, so make use of them in your learning!

Although it takes time to get to know ICT systems, hardware and software, it is an investment of time that is worth the effort. Activity 8.3 will start you off.

Activity 8.3   ICT in the classroom

Talk to your head of department, ICT head of department or systems manager in school to find out what ICT hardware and software is available to you. Complete the table opposite to indicate what is available and to identify any training that you may need.

Activity 8.3 *continued*

Hardware/software available	What this is/could be use for in Design and Technology	Training needed so that I can use it
Interactive/electronic whiteboard		
Data projector system		
PowerPoint		
School network system		
Digital camera/video		
Subject-specific hardware – machinery and equipment		
Subject-specific software		

ICT and administration

ICT now assists with much of a teacher's administrative work; it can be used to record pupil information and assessments, set pupil targets, write reports and analyse pupil data. These are all likely to be part of the school's data management system and you need to find out what systems are used by your school, how to access it, what information is available to you and what information you need to put into the system.

If there is no system, then I suggest you set up spreadsheets on your computer and keep your own records. If you are not sure how to use spreadsheets, there are several guidebooks that will help you or speak to the ICT head of department or technician in your school. Spreadsheets allow you to manipulate class lists, showing high to low marks, average marks and individual pupil data.

GWYNETH OWEN-JACKSON

Activity 8.4 ICT and administration

Talk to your head of department or systems manager in school, find out what data management system is used in the school and note below what it is used for and what implications this has for your own work. Note also any training you may need.

School management system used for:	The implications this has for my own work:	Training I need to help me carry out this role:
Recording/accessing pupil information		
Recording pupil assessments		
Setting pupil targets		
Writing reports		
Analysing pupil data		
Pastoral work		
Other . . .		

Professional development

Subject knowledge in Design and Technology is constantly being updated and you need to keep abreast of this. One way of doing this is through regular reading of relevant websites. Again, it would be difficult to list 'relevant' websites as these will vary, and may change, but some to get you started are shown at the end of the chapter.

In addition, there are sites that will help you develop your professional knowledge. These include the government website www.standards/dfes.gov.uk, from which you can link to a range of other sites with information on current initiatives and topics. There are sites with information on early years teaching, anti-bullying, personalised learning to name just a few. The General Teaching Council for England, www.gtce.org.uk also has information on a range of topics. Through the Learning Academy of the GTCE you can also be accredited for your professional development, see the website for details.

EMERGING DEVELOPMENTS

New technologies will continue to emerge and develop and you will need to keep up to date through reading professional journals and newspapers. Here are some of the developments currently emerging, at least in education.

E-portfolios

There is a growing range of technology being introduced into teaching, such as personal digital assistants (PDAs) and mobile/smart phones, and growing interest in how these can contribute to the development of e-portfolios.

E-portfolios can be used both as a teaching and learning tool and as an assessment tool. In teaching and learning they allow pupils to record a wide range of information in different formats. PDAs and mobile phones allow pupils to take photographs, short videos and voice recordings. Some PDAs will also enable them to sketch onto their device and save and send the work produced. These devices have the potential to provide a richer record of pupils' work and, by doing so, allowing pupils to develop more creativity in their work.

The e-portfolio could then be submitted electronically to the Award Board for assessment. This would not negate the need for practical skills to be developed, but would do away with the time spent on producing 'folders' which often do not capture the fullness or entirety of work done by pupils. At the time of writing no Award Board yet offers this option, but it is a possibility for the future.

Tablet computers

These are smaller than laptops and more portable, they also have the capability to recognise handwriting and transfer it into text. Currently they are too expensive for major use in schools but there may be tablets available for occasional use, such as for out-of-school learning and industrial visits. You might also consider the possibility of purchasing a tablet for your own use, you could make observation notes in the classroom while pupils were working which could then be transferred to pupil records.

Personal digital assistants (PDAs) and smartphones

The ability of these devices to take photographs, videos and voice recordings has already been mentioned in relation to e-portfolios. They can also be used during industrial placements or visits for pupils to record their observations. You could even consider sending text messages to pupils to share information about their work or to send reminder messages about work due in!

MP3 players

While these are often frowned upon in schools, their ubiquitous presence could be used for educational purposes if you recorded your own podcast, for example, you could record instructions for pupils to listen to when they were ready or for those who missed lessons, or you – or other pupils – could record information for revision purposes.

Virtual keyboard

This is a small device that uses laser technology to beam a keyboard onto any appropriate surface, and wireless technology to link it to your computer. This can be used in the classroom for pupils to input data from anywhere in the classroom to a central computer or in areas where a standard keyboard would not be suitable, such as food areas or materials technology workshops.

Digital pens

These are currently available in the USA and will soon be on sale in the UK. These pens need special paper but will record whatever you write and save it for later downloading onto your computer. This could be useful for pupils to keep records or journals, again for working in industrial placements or out-of-school activities.

Web-logs and Wikis

These are two forms of communication that are now available, although I haven't yet found them being used in secondary education. Web-logs (blogs) could be used within an e-portfolio for pupils to record progress or share their thinking; Wikis (interactive web pages) could be used to develop design ideas, find information or share ideas with others.

SUMMARY

This chapter has outlined some of the ways in which you could use ICT to enhance your teaching and make your own workload a bit easier. It has described some of the technologies currently in use in Design and Technology and some emerging technologies. However, ICT never stands still and the main message of this chapter is that ICT can make life better – and lessons more interesting – if you spend a little time becoming familiar with it and keeping your knowledge and skills up to date. It has been suggested (Ofsted 2003) that using ICT can help improve boys' attainment but I believe that ICT, particularly the emerging technologies, can make learning fun and interesting for all pupils.

While cost and availability will also be issues in school, this should not stop you knowing about these technologies and thinking about where you might introduce them into your teaching.

REFERENCE

Ofsted (2003) *Boys' Achievement in Secondary Schools*, HMI 1659, London: Ofsted

FURTHER READING

Becta (2004) *Getting the Most from your Interactive Whiteboard*, Coventry: Becta
Department for Education and Skills (2003) *Embedding ICT @ Secondary*, London: DfES, see also: www.dfes.gov.uk/ictinschools
Leask, M. and Pachler, N. (2005) *Learning to Teach Using ICT in the Secondary School*, London: Routledge

There are also a number of guidebooks available from any good bookshop on using spread-sheets, databases, word-processing packages, desktop publishing and PowerPoint if you need to develop or extend your skills in any of these areas.

WEBSITES

www.bttg.co.uk
www.esa.int
These are websites for textiles technology. In the www.esa.int website, look for the textiles link.

www.crocodile-clips.com
www.theiet.org.uk
These are websites for ECT.

www.data.org.uk
This is the website of the Design and Technology Association, and contains case studies of work in schools, some of which include the use of ICT.

www.design-technology-info
A general website on Design Technology.

www.dtonline.org
www.tep.org.uk
These are websites for materials technology.

www.foodforum.org.uk
www.nutrition.org.uk
These are websites on food technology.

All these websites were accurate at the time of going to press.

Chapter 9   Cross-curricular teaching and learning

JOHN ROBSON

INTRODUCTION

Central to Design and Technology are the activities of designing and making. Consider all that is involved when you design and make something: subject knowledge, practical skills, research, generation and development of ideas, evaluation and testing, and more. Designing is a complex skill that involves communication, research and thinking skills of various kinds. Designers also need to understand values, have awareness of the needs of people and what effects a new product might have, for example, on the environment or on the local communities. When making, technical know-how and scientific knowledge are both appropriate, as are numeracy and being able to solve problems. Designing and making also require an ability to work with people. These are just some examples of the range of skills and knowledge involved in Design and Technology.

There should be no doubt that Design and Technology has the potential to promote aspects of learning across the curriculum and that it does this in a distinctive way, through designing and making processes. Specifically, Design and Technology can promote the learning of:

- literacy;
- numeracy;
- key skills;
- thinking skills;
- personal, social and health education (PSHE);
- citizenship;
- education for sustainable development (ESD).

This chapter explores these areas and highlights the 'where' and 'how' of opportunities for promoting learning across the curriculum. By having an awareness of the potential for this kind of learning you are more likely to plan it into your lessons and give it emphasis in your teaching.

By the end of this chapter you should:

- know about and understand cross-curricular themes;
- be able to identify where and how activities in Design and Technology can contribute to learning in these themes and to other National Curriculum subjects;
- be able to devise units of work which include cross-curricular links;
- in your teaching of Design and Technology, be able to provide appropriate emphasis in order to promote learning in other areas of the curriculum.

LITERACY

The aim of the National Literacy Strategy in England (see www.standards.dfes.gov.uk) was to provide primary pupils with the literacy skills that would assist their achievement in the secondary school. The National Curriculum also requires secondary teachers to consider the *use of language across the curriculum*; this indicates that aspects of language should be considered in all subjects and specifically it defines what pupils should be taught in relation to:

- writing;
- speaking;
- listening;
- reading.

In Design and Technology, written language is used among other things for annotating drawings, writing reports and evaluations.

Activity 9.1   Use of written language

Think about a design and make activity that you have taught or observed. List examples of where written language was used and suggest where it could have been introduced or extended.

Year group: ....
Topic: ....

Examples of the use of written language	Suggestions for where written language could have been introduced or extended

---

Figure 9.1 Word display board

It is probably true that in Design and Technology we do not spend enough time just *talking about* products. This would allow pupils to express opinions and ideas about their own work, and that of others, and listen to the views of other pupils. However, it is also true that much time is spent on *talking out* design ideas between pupil and teacher, such as when an accurate and detailed description of a design is required; how it is intended to look, work and be made. Here the pupil has to articulate ideas further and this helps to clarify and move ideas on. This is an important phase of pupils' design processes and for literacy learning this *talking out* of design ideas assists the acquisition and use of vocabulary.

Technical vocabulary is essential to operating effectively within the subject. Pupils need to recognise, understand and use language appropriately in order to:

- express ideas – *design specification, concept model, aesthetics*;
- discuss materials, equipment, processes and properties – *vacuum forming, sublimation printing, laser, denaturation, ductile*;
- describe products – *caramelised, flexible, texture*;
- evaluate – *better than because . . ., compromise, modification, meets the requirement, criteria*.

Boys' under-achievement has been linked to their poor literacy skills (Ofsted 2003) and by encouraging their technical vocabulary you could contribute to improving boys' written and spoken English, thus improving their overall results.

One way to help encourage the use of technical vocabulary is to print out appropriate words and phrases onto cards, using a large font size, and put them onto a wall display or use them in classroom activities, as illustrated in Figure 9.1.

NUMERACY

The National Numeracy Strategy (see www.standards.dfes.gov.uk) was introduced to improve numeracy skills and examined how subjects might link with the National Curriculum requirements for mathematics. Opportunities for the use and development of numeracy skills are easily found in Design and Technology, for example:

- working with accuracy;
- measuring – length, weight, electric current, temperature;
- mathematical modelling – force diagrams for structures, nutritional spreadsheets;
- making calculations;
- collecting and using data;
- using graphs and charts.

Can you think of other opportunities in lessons you have observed or taught?

Activity 9.2   Developing numeracy skills

Using the lesson planning pro-forma provided by your school or training provider, plan a focused task for pupils to develop specific, identified, numeracy skills. It will help pupils' learning if the task is 'real' and associated with their design and make activity. Teach the task and evaluate pupils' learning of the identified numeracy skills.

KEY SKILLS

The National Curriculum sets out in general terms how all subjects can promote common areas of learning known as *key skills* and these are discussed in *Learning to Teach Design and Technology in the Secondary School* (Owen-Jackson, 2007).

Activity 9.3   Focus on key skills

As you observe a series of lessons being taught, or plan your own lessons, note the opportunities that arise for pupils to develop key skills: communication or IT skills, working with others, improving own learning or solving problems.

Lesson Year group/topic	Opportunities for key skills communication/IT skills – working with others – improving own learning – problem solving (state the key skill and how this was developed)

When you have completed Activity 9.3, think about how you can incorporate opportunities for pupils to develop key skills into your own lessons. Make these opportunities explicit in your planning.

THINKING SKILLS

The Key Stage 3 National Strategy (now the Secondary Strategy) highlighted the need to teach thinking skills. Design and Technology lessons can contribute significantly to these:

- *information processing* – this is essential for effective research, *where* to find relevant information and *how* it can be used. Editing, sorting, classifying, seeing relationships, comparing and re-presenting information are all involved. Information gathered needs to be used judiciously, a skill which pupils need to learn and practise.
- *reasoning* – pupils need to justify their judgements and decisions with reasons. Reasons should be based on evidence which pupils can point out. Reasoning skills are especially important when analysing and evaluating.
- *enquiry* – the ability to ask relevant questions, know how to research, anticipate outcomes and, as a result, plan what to do. Enquiry skills will help to pose problems as well as to further define existing ones. When designing, it is frequently useful to pose *what if* questions.
- *creative thinking* – Design and Technology has much to contribute to the development of pupils' creativity. Through using imagination and creative thinking, pupils are able to generate and extend ideas; sudden insights and unusual connections can be stimulated which lead to real innovation.
- *evaluative and analytical skills* – these enable pupils to make judgements about finished products. Such skills are also invaluable when gathering information – knowing what is of use, deriving conclusions from testing and making judgements about the value of what they do and hear. Developing and applying appropriate criteria are also key.

Focused tasks and design and make assignments (DMAs) can provide an excellent vehicle for the development of different types of thinking, but only if you plan for them.

One school has developed a number of starter/plenary activities that support the development of pupils' thinking skills, these include:

- *What is this?* – pupils are given a number of statements that relate to a particular topic and asked to rank them in order of importance or classify them, using their own headings. This leads to a discussion about the purpose and value of information and develops 'information-processing' skills.
- *Why did you do that?* – pupils are asked to state, or write, one process or decision that they carried out in the lesson. They then have to justify the use of that process or the decision made, in relation to their own work. This helps to develop 'reasoning' skills.

PERSONAL, SOCIAL AND HEALTH EDUCATION (PSHE)

This concerns knowledge and practical skills which help pupils to live healthily and to deal with spiritual, moral, social and cultural issues. The knowledge, skills and understanding are defined under three main headings:

- *Developing confidence and responsibility and making the most of their abilities.* In Design and Technology pupils develop confidence through achieving success with the products they design and make. Responsibility is developed through working in shared environments and through designing for other people. During design and make processes pupils should be encouraged to develop and make the most of their abilities.

- *Developing a healthy, safer lifestyle.* What constitutes a healthy diet, nutrition and making healthy food products form important aspects within food technology. This also links with the Healthy Schools Programme (see www.wiredforhealth.gov.uk and www.foodinschools.org), which is involving food technology in helping pupils know, understand and apply the principles of healthy eating in their own lives. In all areas pupils are made aware of the health and safety issues surrounding the use of materials and equipment.
- *Developing good relationships and respecting the differences between people.* Opportunities arise when pupils are required to work in groups or when they are designing for people with particular or special needs. Assignments can also have different cultural starting points.

How Design and Technology promotes pupils' spiritual, moral, social and cultural development is not always easily understood. Some aspects of how it does this are indicated above but it is worth considering these further:

- *spiritual development* – while it may be difficult to make any straightforward connections, pupils should be made aware of and be able to recognise material and non-material needs; for the latter, an awareness of meaning and purpose in life and of differing values is important. Helping pupils to recognise imagination and its role in designing is also relevant here.
- *moral development* – moral decisions are involved where there are both benefits and disadvantages for makers and users and this is promoted by encouraging pupils to think about the effects that products might have on individuals, the environment and society, as in education for sustainable development (see below). In particular, pupils should consider what effects the introduction of new technologies and systems might have.
- *social development* – when designing, pupils will consider the needs and views of others. Social development is also promoted through group work, discussions and through role-play in simulation exercises.
- *cultural development* – this is supported by using a study of other cultures and customs as starting points for DMAs and by pupils exploring the role of artefacts and their effects within different cultures.

CITIZENSHIP

The focus for citizenship is on the place and the responsibilities of the individual within society. It is about pupils developing in a way that enables them to take their place as informed and responsible citizens. The framework for citizenship defines three areas of knowledge, skills and understanding:

- *knowledge and understanding about becoming informed citizens* – under this heading pupils are required to be taught about political, economic, environmental, and social implications of the world as a global community. Design and Technology can contribute to this if pupils are required to consider the economic, environmental and social effects of made products and their own designs.
- *developing skills of enquiry and communication* – these are central to designing. There are also many opportunities within Design and Technology for pupils to contribute to group and class discussions or debates in the exploration of ideas and concepts.
- *developing skills of participation and responsible action* – in a design and make activity, this is exactly what pupils will be doing. 'Real context' assignments provide good opportunities for pupils to work with real clients, community groups or industry.

There are many ways in which lessons can be adapted to incorporate aspects of citizenship, for example:

- asking pupils to research legislation and consumer rights in relation to specific products/services;
- incorporating economic, environmental or social values into design briefs;
- researching 'fair trade' issues;
- product analysis, using products from other cultures or traditions; this could also be used as a starting point for a new design brief.

EDUCATION FOR SUSTAINABLE DEVELOPMENT (ESD)

Concerns over the way we live and for the future of our planet lead to a real and increasing need for ESD. It provides an approach to the whole curriculum and promotes a particular ethos in the management of schools. The National Curriculum (www.nc.net) states that ESD will help people to participate in decisions about the way we do things individually and collectively that improve the quality of life without damaging the planet for the future.

Design and Technology has a clear and significant role in promoting ESD since at its core is the idea of effecting change in products and systems which lead to improvements. The subject prepares future designers and technologists who have a particular responsibility in ensuring that we live sustainably. Equally, it educates future consumers.

The issues involved in sustainability can be complex; they involve not only environmental considerations, but also social, cultural and economic ones. These issues inter-relate and often contradict, therefore moral decisions have to be made. The issues, however, can be introduced into Design and Technology through simple tasks and activities. Once introduced, sustainability should become a normal consideration in all designing and making activities which pupils undertake. Together with function and aesthetics, sustainability is a principle against which to judge what constitutes 'good design'.

The resources available to support ESD are growing but, as with all resources, you will need to consider the suitability of those recommended for the learning objectives you have planned. You will also need to consider whether they are appropriate for your school and pupils. Some resources to start you off are Practical Action/DATA (2005) and ITDG (2000). See also the websites:

www.practicalaction.org; www.stepin.org and www.sda-uk.org

Activity 9.4   Assessing products for sustainability

Go to the website www.sda-uk.org, enter the Students site and select Tools. From there you can download a copy of the 'eco-design web'. Using the pro-forma provided by your school or training provider, plan a focused task in which pupils use this tool to determine how sustainable some products are. If possible, teach this focused task, have the product examples available for pupils to handle, and invite pupils to suggest what the completed webs tell them. Evaluate how successful this task was in raising pupils' awareness of sustainability issues.

OTHER SUBJECTS AND ASPECTS

Design and Technology also has links with other National Curriculum subjects. The relationships with art and design and science are clear, for example, as a way of stimulating design ideas for jewellery, pupils might study a style or movement in art, and understanding about both nutrition or technical textiles involves science. By looking at cultural and historical differences, or the development of technologies and systems over time, links with geography, history and religious studies can also be made.

Other cross-curricular aspects include:

- *financial capability* – deciding what, and how much of, materials and components to use; working to budgets;
- *enterprise* – designing and making a product that meets a need and then marketing and selling it. Groups of pupils often work together as small 'companies'.
- *work-related learning* – visiting speakers from industry; visits to companies and work experience placements and careers talks.

Activity 9.5   Learning links

Obtain a copy of a Key Stage 4 scheme of work that you will be teaching. Read through it and identify opportunities for learning in cross-curricular themes (financial capability, enterprise, work-related learning). Note where and how you could incorporate these opportunities and annotate the scheme. With the agreement of your school-based tutor, teach the amended lessons and evaluate their effectiveness in raising pupils' awareness of the identified issues.

Year group .... Topic	
Opportunities to teach financial capability:	
Where:	How:
Opportunities to teach enterprise:	
Where:	How:
Opportunities to teach work-related learning:	
Where:	How:

SUMMARY

The standards for qualified teacher status require you to understand and implement the cross-curricular expectations of the National Curriculum. While Design and Technology has a valuable contribution to make, this will not happen unless you plan for it, and this chapter should have helped you see how you can do that. Beyond this, though, you should continue to recognise and use opportunities for cross-curricular learning. One benefit of improving pupils' cross-curricular learning is that it is likely to lead to improvements in the quality of their work in the subject itself.

REFERENCES

ITDG (2000) *Live Well, Live Wisely! Technology for Sustainable Development*, London: ITDG

Ofsted (2003) *Boys' Achievement in Secondary Schools*, London: Ofsted

Practical Action/DATA (2005) *Sustainability in Design and Technology: A Guide for Teachers and Teacher Trainers*, Bourton-on-Dunsmore: Practical Action/DATA

FURTHER READING

DfEE (1995) *Design and Technology: Characteristics of Good Practice in Secondary Schools*, London: HMSO

DfEE/QCA (1999) *The National Curriculum: Handbook for Secondary Teachers in England*, London: HMSO

DfES (2004a) *KS3 National Strategy: Literacy in Design and Technology*, London: HMSO

DfES (2004b) *KS3 National Strategy: Foundation subjects: design and technology: Framework and Training Materials*, London: HMSO

Owen-Jackson, G. (2000) *Learning to Teach Design and Technology in the Secondary School*, London: Routledge

School Curriculum and Assessment Authority (SCAA) (1997) *The Contribution of Design and Technology to the Curriculum*, London: SCAA

Teacher Training Agency (TTA) (2005) *Qualify to Teach: Handbook of Guidance*, London: TTA

WEBSITES

www.data.org.uk

www.nc.uk.net

www.standards.dfes.gov.uk

www.tre.ngfl.gov.uk

Chapter 10 Creating an effective learning environment

FRANK BANKS

INTRODUCTION

'I hate this place – it smells!' However long one has been teaching, certain pupils will always be remembered; that frequent refrain of Cathy's sulky entrance to the workshop still echoes in my memory many years on. She had a point. The science and technology area of the school certainly had some interesting aromas caused by the close proximity of laboratories to workshops and the mingling smells of gas, glue and gunk. The workroom environment, I admit, left much to be desired and I expect many other less vocal pupils were also affected by it.

I quickly came to realise that the physical environment for Design and Technology is very important. Not only does it affect our attitude to the subject, it also has a profound effect on learning. The layout of the room itself says much about the way that the teacher relates to pupils and how pupils can relate to each other. The safe distribution, use and collection of tools and resources in an efficient and controlled manner contribute significantly to appropriate pupil behaviour. If pupils can take responsibility for their work and make informed choices of tools and components as they progress through a task, they are better able to take control of their own learning. But if they have to wait for equipment, materials or attention, pupils become bored and frustrated and sometimes disruptive. In creating an effective learning environment, there is a very close link between the class layout, resource management, behaviour management and the safety of all who are in the workshop.

By the end of this chapter you should be able to:

- understand how the physical environment can affect pupils' learning;
- evaluate the systems for distribution and collection of tools and materials in your school;
- understand how the physical environment and the management of resources impact on the behaviour of the pupils;
- understand how the behaviour of pupils combined with the appropriate use of tools and resources impacts on the health and safety of all.

ROOM LAYOUT

Obviously there are different requirements for rooms in the different focus areas of Design and Technology, for example, the spaces needed around a pillar-drill in a materials technology workshop, the table 'footprint' needed for textiles work and access to allow for cleaning work surfaces in food technology all require different responses. In all areas, however, there is a requirement for dust-free spaces for folio work and space needs to be found for ICT work to be carried out. In addition, the introduction of new equipment over the years may have changed the original, planned, layout.

Activity 10.1 asks you to think about the space in which you teach, use the school in which you currently work or one that you know well.

Activity 10.1 Considering furniture, fittings, fitness and facility

Think of a Design and Technology room that you know well. Draw a plan view of the position of the tables or benches, the services such as electricity and water and the position of the places where tools, equipment and materials can be accessed. On the plan, indicate the position where the pupils and the teacher usually start the lesson.

Activity 10.1 *continued*

If possible, compare your completed plan with that of a colleague who teaches in a different material area and answer the following questions:

What differences do you notice?

What changes would you make to your room layout following discussion with your colleague?

When you are in school, discuss the room layout with your mentor. What do they think about the room layout?

The Teachernet Design and Technology website has a number of example layouts of rooms (www.teachernet.gov.uk/designandtechnology/). Look at the plans on the website and compare them with your sketch. Does this change any of your responses to the questions in Activity 10.1?

The location of the tables or benches can reveal the expectations you have for pupil interaction in your lessons.

Activity 10.2 A pupil-activity brainstorm

Working first on your own, and then in consultation with another Design and Technology teacher, brainstorm different activities where pupils work individually, in pairs or small groups, as a whole class and as a group of classes. Use the template on the following page.

My guess is that it was very easy to think of lessons when pupils work on their own. The manufacture of an individual artefact that a pupil can take home is a key part of most schemes of work. Discussion work in pairs or small groups is vital too if pupils are to address values implicit in products and the impact the product and materials have on society and the environment. The pupils will work as a whole class for presentations and evaluations and perhaps with other groups if there is a guest speaker or a whole-school 'challenge'. In some schools, the timetable is collapsed at certain times of the year to allow for a concentrated period of Design and Technology work.

The extent to which you were able to think of different ways that pupils interact in your lessons has much to do with how you think pupils learn and how you wish to be viewed as a teacher. Environmental psychology is a discipline that draws on areas of knowledge such as geography, architecture, sociology, anthropology and – most significantly for technology teachers – design and ergonomics. Norman (1998) points out that everyday objects are not only physical but have an impact on how we relate to the world. The ability of a pupil to sit to work, move around the room (or not) and the nature and usefulness of display material have a profound effect on their creativity and ability to work constructively with others.

Activity 10.2 *continued*

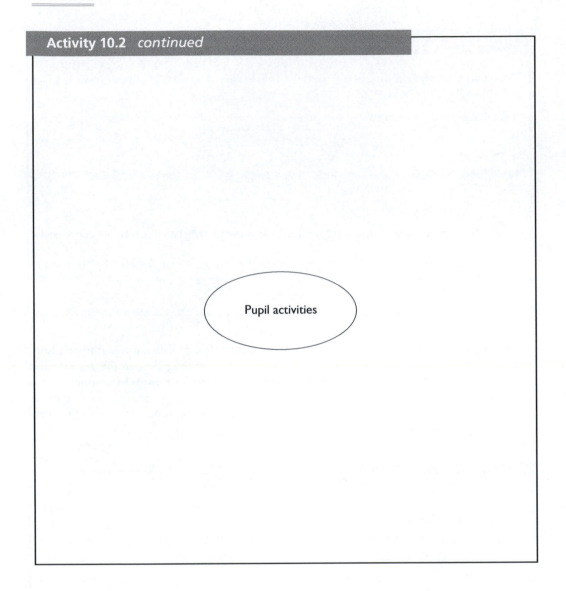

Storage systems too can hinder as well as help in the efficient conduct of tasks. According to Norman (ibid., pp. 189–200), design should help pupils to understand the classroom environment and what is expected of them. This would involve:

- avoiding unnecessary complexity in the tasks pupils have to undertake;
- providing visible memory aids and feedback;
- developing automatic routines;
- using appropriate technologies with a critical eye for gains and losses;
- maintaining elements of control in the details of actions as well as the overall direction of the task or project of learning;
- planning enough flexibility to allow errors and learning from errors.

As teachers of design, there is much that our subject knowledge could contribute to an improved learning environment. Recent research into 'brain-based learning' (Smith and Call 1999; Ginnis 2002; Smith 2002) brings together some of the issues we have considered so far – the physical environment of the Design and Technology room and the way that teachers and pupils interact with each other in that environment. Smith summarises this into nine principles (Smith and Call 1999, pp. 33–4, adapted here), shown in Table 10.1.

Table 10.1 Brain-based learning principles

1	The brain develops best in environments with high levels of sensory stimulation and cognitive challenge.
2	Optimal conditions for learning involve sustained levels of cognitive challenge with low threat.
3	Higher order intellectual activity may decrease in environments the learner considers emotionally or physiologically hostile (remember Cathy in the Introduction!).
4	The brain thrives on immediacy of feedback and choice.
5	There are recognised processing centres in the hemispheres of the brain. This suggests structured activities.
6	Each brain has a high degree of plasticity, developing and integrating classroom with other experiences.
7	Learning takes place at a number of levels. This requires a range of strategies and personal goals.
8	Memory is a series of processes rather than locations. To access long-term memory is an active not a passive process.
9	Humans are 'hard-wired' for a language response. Discussion is a vital part of learning.

There is a close inter-relationship between learning and the physical space in which pupils work. The space can stimulate and encourage individual and collaborative working which provides a welcome practical alternative to a school diet which over-emphasises the academic. Try to ensure that your learning environment is of this kind and not cold, dirty or unwelcoming.

Activity 10.3 Display – dusty drawings or dazzling demonstrations?

On the plan sketch of your Design and Technology room drawn in Activity 10.1 note down where any displays such as posters, models or pictures are located. How often are they changed? How many of them are pupils' work?

RESOURCE MANAGEMENT AND SAFE WORKING

We have considered the general Design and Technology environment and now turn to the organisation of resources within that space. If pupils are to gain maximum benefit in the Design and Technology workroom, they must know where to find the tools and equipment they need. Activity 10.4 will help you to consider how effective this is in the room in which you work.

Activity 10.4 An audit of resources

Returning to the Design and Technology room plan you used for Activity 10.1, complete the table on the following page, either from memory or when in school, detailing the location of materials, tools and equipment.

Activity 10.4 *continued*

Questions	Detailed answers
Layout and siting Is there a natural flow between processes to reduce movement? Are all tools/equipment easily and safely accessible to all pupils?	
Safety equipment Is safety equipment, such as oven gloves or goggles, close to the relevant equipment?	
Storing hand tools/equipment Are tools/equipment which are used regularly stored in racks or trays associated with each working area? Are any cutting edges protected and do they have an easy 'home' for storage? Are handles colour-coded so that each set of tools/equipment is easily checked by pupils themselves? Are tools which are used less frequently stored for easy access with each having an easily identified location?	
Storing materials Are offcuts of metals, plastics, wood and textiles stored in the work area itself? What containers are used to store and give access to small items such as electronic components, cotton reels, pencils, rulers and erasers? Are separate storage rooms available for the storage of wood, metals, textiles, food ingredients? Are they secure? Are lengths of wood or metal stored vertically for easy access? How are they racked? Is sheet material stored on its edge and located for easy removal? Are textiles stored horizontally or vertically? Are they accessible, and safe?	
Storing consumable materials How do pupils gain access to consumable materials? Are small quantities of items such as adhesives and solder, labelled and sensibly located? Are perishable food ingredients stored in suitable conditions? Is there sufficient storage of the right kind for food ingredients?	

Your answers to these questions will call to mind expectations we have about pupils working autonomously. It is common in all areas of Design and Technology to colour-code sets of tools or utensils that are used every lesson as this helps to ensure that pupils have all they need at the start and can easily check that all is there at the end of the lesson. Tools borrowed from a cupboard can be easily checked if a silhouette of each item is painted to show where it should go. Williams (1994) recommends that this is done in a light colour rather than black as on a dark wet Friday the silhouette can be mistaken for the tool! He summarises some basic practices which will help ensure a self-disciplined and safe working environment (ibid., p. 11), see Table 10.2.

Table 10.2 Creating a safe working environment

	Recommended procedure
	Training
✓	No pupil should use any machine/equipment until proper training has been given. Even then, its use must be under reasonable but careful supervision with the correct safety aids and procedure being used
✓	Two pupils should not be at the same machine together, as it is possible that one of the pupils will start the machine before the other is ready
	Carrying tools
✓	Hand tools that have to be carried around the workroom should, if possible, be placed in racks or trays. If an individual tool has to be carried and it has a sharp point or cutting edge (for example, scissors, knives, chisels) it should be held with three fingers and the thumb around the handle and the forefinger pointing down the blade, it should be held pointing downwards and close to the outside of the thigh. If this safety rule is always insisted upon, accidents caused by pupils falling over or brushing against each other when holding dangerous tools will be eliminated
✓	Pupils should be strongly encouraged to pick up chisels, awls, screwdrivers and similar tools with both hands, and to use them with both hands until they are replaced on the bench or in the rack. It is then impossible for any of the fingers to come in contact with a sharp edge
	Soldering irons and hot objects
✓	Pupils using hot objects such as pans and soldering irons should always place them on a stand after use so that no one is tempted to touch the heated part.
✓	With processes involving the heating of metal, such as annealing or enamelling, pupils should be reminded to place the hot metal on a heat-resistant mat and to treat any object on that mat with extreme caution. This area should be permanently labelled 'hot-work' or something similar. Common-sense precautions of this sort will make accidents in the design and technology room a rare occurrence

BEHAVIOUR FOR LEARNING

Throughout this chapter we have emphasised the interrelationship between the working environment, the efficiency in distribution of tools and materials, the consequent behaviour of pupils and the quality of their learning. We are now going to consider some specific aspects of 'behaviour management'.

You will not be short of advice on how to manage difficult pupils – and every teacher, however experienced, will meet pupils with challenging behaviour. Such advice is very helpful, it illustrates that there is no one 'right' way to respond and that much poor behaviour is context-specific. However, some 'advice' can be unhelpful, such as that which involves negative labelling when you are told, 'Watch that one, I taught his brother.'

Activity 10.5   Critical incidents

Every teacher recalls an incident with a pupil that they feel they could have handled better. Maybe it led to a confrontation. Maybe, with hindsight, a comment was made that made the pupil feel foolish, resentful or angry which may not have led to misbehaviour but was counter-productive in terms of relationships and the pupil's attitude to the subject.

Think of an incident that you have been involved in or witnessed either as a teacher or a pupil. Write brief notes below about the incident and discuss this with your mentor.

Think of an incident that you have been involved in or witnessed either as a teacher or a pupil. Write brief notes here about the incident.

When in school discuss the incident with your mentor and ask them to suggest alternative responses, which you can note here.

The Teachernet website has some helpful information on behaviour management (http://www.teachernet.gov.uk/supplyteachers/). For example, it notes that pupils who demonstrate inappropriate behaviours 'will have the often subconscious aim' of:

- attracting attention;
- demonstrating power;
- seeking revenge;
- escaping by withdrawal.

While poor behaviour is not solely due to boys, they are more likely than girls to present you with challenge. You need to develop appropriate strategies, following school policy and procedure, for responding to this and Ofsted (2003) have suggested that boys respond well to a consistent and fair approach to discipline and to teachers who set clear limits and have high expectations. Boys often work well in Design and Technology and you can reinforce this through the use of a variety of activities, short-term targets and feedback. Discipline problems are also reduced if you can develop good relationships with pupils, boys and girls, as pupils work better for teachers they like. This does not mean that you have to become a 'friend' to them; most pupils state that they like teachers who are firm and fair, who explain clearly, who show enthusiasm for their subject and who have a sense of humour.

Since the Elton Report (DES 1989), schools have worked to establish behaviour policies which encourage good behaviour rather than simply punishing bad. In addition, a rational approach based on understanding some key times where problems might occur is useful.

Beginnings of lessons

- Try to arrive before the class.
- Always make sure that the class is quiet, with bags put away and coats off before you begin.
- Have some stimulus to set the class going, such as one of the starter activities mentioned in Chapter 12.
- Keep the introduction short and, if you need to impart an extended amount of information, use a resource in addition to talking.
- Make the first pupil activities clear and straightforward; avoid being overwhelmed early in a lesson by a multitude of questions about how something is to be done.
- Be clear about the sequence of activities, 'what happens next' (detailed lesson planning helps, see Chapter 12).
- Be aware that latecomers may interrupt your introduction; have a form of words that asks them to sit down and wait and that you will clarify what has to be done once the lesson is underway.

Transitions within lessons

- Prepare the resources for a transition in advance; valuable teaching time can be lost if you or the pupils disappear into a cupboard!
- Ensure pupils are warned in advance that a change of activity is impending.
- Be wary of transitions that change the atmosphere of the class too abruptly. As an experienced teacher you will be able to handle this, even using it as a technique; as a novice, it can cause problems.
- If the transitions are to be individual or group rather than class-based, then the ground rules or procedures for making a change must be clearly set out.

Endings of lessons

- Find ways in which some of the `ending tasks' can begin well in advance of the end of the class; you may find ways of collecting up folios and equipment yourself as you go around talking to pupils.
- Ensure that the ending of the lesson is not too overcrowded; don't, for example, try to summarise the lesson, collect equipment, set homework and leave the room tidy, all in the space of two or three minutes.
- Plan an appropriate plenary activity (see Chapter 12).
- Revise your lesson plan if the time pupils take over certain activities is longer than you thought; don't try to rush through important concepts in five minutes merely in order to ensure you've fulfilled your lesson plan.
- In most circumstances a moment of quiet before the class leaves, and a word of commendation in the context of thinking about what they've achieved, creates a pattern and routine that can be helpful and relaxing.

SUMMARY

In this chapter we have considered the way that an effective learning environment is created by an interplay between the physical space, which should be inviting and rich, with the way that a teacher uses that space and the resources available to work with the pupils. With some straightforward thought to the physical and human interactions that will occur, much can be done to make Design and Technology workrooms among the most stimulating and creative environments for learning for all pupils.

REFERENCES

DES (1989) *Discipline in Schools* (The Elton Report), London: DES

Ginnis, P. (2002) *The Teacher's Toolkit*, Camarthen: Crown House Publishing

Norman, D.A. (1998) *The Design of Everyday Things*, London: MIT Press

Ofsted (2003) *Boys' Achievement in Secondary Schools*, London: Ofsted

Smith, A. (2002) *The Brain's Behind It*, Stafford: Network Educational Press

Smith, A. and Call, P. (1999) *The ALPS Approach*, Stafford: Network Educational Press

Williams, P. (1994) *Working with Resistant Materials*, Milton Keynes: Open University Press

FURTHER READING

Curry, M. (2000) *Building a Peaceful School*, Lichfield: NASEN

Daniels, H., Visser, J. *et al.* (1998) *Emotional and Behavioural Difficulties in Mainstream School.* Research Report RR90, London: DfEE

HMSO (2004) *Design and Technology Accommodation in Secondary Schools: A Design Guide*, London: TSO

WEBSITES

http://www.teachernet.gov.uk/supplyteachers/volume.cfm?&vid=4
This is the Teachernet Behaviour Management website.

http://www.teachernet.gov.uk/designandtechnology/1_home.cfm?id=4010
This is the Teachernet Design and Technology website.

Chapter 11   Assessing pupils' learning

GWYNETH OWEN-JACKSON

INTRODUCTION

One of the key messages of this book is that you should be continually thinking about ways to improve your teaching in order to maximise pupils' learning, and understanding and using effective assessment practices contributes a great deal to this. Assessment has always been considered as part of education, pupils down the ages have been tested on what they have learnt. Current practice, however, is moving away from the traditional model of assessment as a final measurement of learning, i.e summative assessment, to assessment becoming part of the learning process itself, i.e. formative assessment or assessment for learning. This chapter considers assessment for learning in some detail and how you can incorporate this into your practice; it also considers how summative assessment is carried out and what this contributes to pupils' learning.

By the end of this chapter you should:

- understand how assessment for learning contributes to pupils' learning;
- know a range of assessment strategies;
- be aware of the role of summative assessment in pupils' learning.

WHY ASSESS?

Assessment serves several purposes, these are explored in *Learning to Teach Design and Technology in the Secondary School* (Owen-Jackson, 2007) and you should look at that before you proceed with this chapter.

It is important for you to be clear about the purposes of assessment because *why* you are doing it should influence *what* and *how* you assess. A discussion of assessment in Design and Technology cannot ignore the issue of *what* is being assessed. Design and Technology, particularly as defined by the National Curriculum in England and in examination spec-ifications, is described as a *process*, with pupils learning how to carry out processes such as planning, researching, designing, communicating, making and evaluating and, in doing this, they apply the knowledge and skills they have learnt. In contrast, much of the assessment that occurs is assessment only *of* pupils' knowledge and skills, what they know and what they can do. It is important, therefore, to consider how we can assess pupils' *capability* in Design and Technology, i.e. their ability in carrying out the processes and applying knowledge and skills appropriately.

One of the purposes of assessment, some would argue the main purpose, is to promote further learning; so how does this influence what and how you assess?

ASSESSMENT FOR LEARNING (AfL)

As the name suggests, assessment for learning (AfL) provides evidence of pupils' current level of knowledge, skill or capability and uses the evidence to plan the next step or stages of learning. This should indicate to you that AfL is part of the planning process and should not be considered in isolation, assessment information should inform your planning and teaching.

Where do I start?

The starting point is knowing what the pupils already know and can do. You will find this information from a range of sources, for example:

- Key Stage 2 data – particularly useful in Year 7. There are not national data for Design and Technology at KS2 so subject-specific information is likely to be from teacher assessments, you should try to find out how these were conducted;
- data from earlier units completed by the pupils – useful when starting a new unit of work;
- teacher assessment data from Year 9 – useful in Year 10;
- predicted examination grades – useful in Year 11 and Year 13.

Note that some of the data result from summative assessment, tests and examinations, so that summative assessment becomes a part of and informs formative assessment procedures, identified by Black *et al.* (2002) as an important aspect.

In addition, you will need to access information the school holds about any pupils with special needs or those on the gifted and talented register.

In many schools, pupil data are held on a computer system, which makes accessing it much easier. If such a system operates in your school, you need to find how you can input data if required, for example at the end of a unit of work.

Activity 11.1 Accessing data

In your school, find out what pupil data are available and access as much of this as you can. You may need to talk to your mentor, the Special Needs Co-ordinator (SENCO) and/or a member of senior management. Compile as much data as you can for the year groups or classes that you teach and make reference to it when planning lessons.

Then what?

Having data is only the first part of the process of assessment for learning processes, the next is using the data to decide what pupils need to do next. The assessment data should give you an indication of the levels at which classes or pupils are working so that you can plan lessons that will move them forward; consider also whether you need to provide support for pupils working below these levels or extension/enrichment work for pupils working above them. In addition, do the data indicate that you need to plan for pupils with special needs, such as dyslexia, physical difficulties, English as an additional language or other learning difficulties? Lesson planning is discussed in detail in Chapter 12.

Your lesson plan should also indicate how you will assess pupils to ensure that they are making progress and achieving the planned learning objectives.

ASSESSING IN DESIGN AND TECHNOLOGY LESSONS

Many student teachers think that Design and Technology lessons, especially practical lessons, are too busy to incorporate assessment opportunities, but this is not the case. You need to plan assessment into your lesson, so what could you do? Black *et al.* (2002) identified important aspects of AfL as:

- using questioning as an assessment technique;
- providing effective feedback;
- using peer and self-assessment;
- using summative assessment outcomes to inform AfL.

Questioning is an important teaching and assessment strategy and you should not leave it to chance. When lesson planning, first consider why you are questioning, is it to check pupils' factual knowledge, to extend their thinking, to engage them or some other purpose? Second, consider what questions would be appropriate. Questions can be closed or open. Closed questions are those that require only a short answer, usually right or wrong, such as 'What type of saw is this'?; they are used to check knowledge. Open questions can have a variety of answers and require pupils to think more deeply, for example, 'Why have you selected pine to make your (product)?' When planning questions, make sure that you include both open and closed questions and that you plan questions to challenge pupils to use higher-order thinking, for example, asking them to analyse, evaluate or justify.

The way in which you ask questions can also help or hinder pupils' learning. You should

- make the question clear;
- give pupils time to think about the answer;
- provide prompts if necessary, or re-phrase the question;
- respond sensitively to incorrect answers, use them to get to the correct answer;
- aim specific questions at specific pupils.

As well as responding to questions asked by you, encourage pupils to ask questions as these can be an indicator of their level of understanding or thinking.

Activity 11.2   Questioning as assessment for learning

Take a lesson plan that you have taught, or will be teaching, and read through to see if it includes the planned use of questions. If it does, then check if you have used a range of open and closed questions and questions to promote higher order thinking. If not, then annotate the plan to show where questions could have been included – and note what the pupils' responses would have told you about their level of understanding.

Other strategies that would give you assessment information include:

- written or graphical work – whether classwork or homework, this is an obvious tool for assessment;
- practical outcomes – again, an obvious tool, but remember to monitor outcomes as they progress, not just at the end;
- discussions pupil/teacher and pupil/pupil – as with questions, teacher or pupil-led discussions can reveal pupils' understanding and thinking;

- starter/plenary activities – planned activities such as quizzes or question-and-answer sessions can reveal pupils' learning from previous lessons or activities;
- pupil presentations – giving pupils opportunities to present their work, whether this be research, design work or manufactured products, can be useful.

When lesson planning, it will help if you can indicate where assessment opportunities occur alongside the learning to remind yourself that you need to be assessing!

Activity 11.3 Planning assessment opportunities

Think about a lesson that you have to plan for, if this is not appropriate, then think about a lesson that you have taught or observed being taught. If your existing planning pro-forma does not include a section on 'assessment opportunities' then amend it as shown in Figure 11.1. Plan your lesson to show where assessment opportunities occur and what assessment strategies you will, or could, use. Try to include a range of assessment methods in your lessons so that you expand the range that you are familiar with. If possible, teach the lesson and evaluate the effectiveness of the assessments.

Having planned the assessment opportunities, you need to be clear about the criteria that you will use when you make your assessments. These criteria should then be shared with pupils so that they know what you are expecting of them; this has been shown to be effective in helping to raise the standard of pupils' work, particularly with older pupils. Assessment criteria can be displayed, together with examples of high quality work, and pupils can be referred to these while working.

Activity 11.4 asks you to think about planning appropriate assessment criteria for pupils working at different levels.

Whatever activity pupils engage in, if they are to learn from it, then it will be important that you provide them with feedback; this could be written feedback on their work or oral feedback within a lesson. Research by Black *et al.* (2002) indicated that effective teacher feedback has certain features:

- it focuses on the quality of pupils' work rather than presentation or other issues;
- it is specific to the task undertaken;
- it relates to the learning objectives of the lesson;
- it is positive and identifies what is good as well as what could be improved;
- it identifies what the pupil needs to do to improve.

For example, telling a pupil that they have done 'good work' is not helpful as it does not let them know what was good. A more helpful comment would be: 'You have produced some good designs and annotated them well, as you were asked to do, but you have not always considered the criteria. Look again at your designs and add notes to say how well each meets the criteria.'

Peer assessment, asking pupils to assess each other's work, has been identified as a useful strategy but care needs to be taken to ensure that pupils understand what is being assessed and the criteria for assessment, and you need to build up their skills in peer assessment through introducing activities over a period of time. You can begin by asking them to assess the work of anonymous pupils from previous years or other classes, and guide them in how to do this. Pupils can then be asked to give one positive point and one area for improvement for a piece of work. Over time, pupils can develop agreed assessment criteria for peer assessment.

Date/time	Lesson no.	Class	Room ....
No. in class: .... girls .... boys		Current NC levels *insert here information from your assessment data*	
Focus area:		Topic:	
Link to NC/examination specification:			
Learning objectives:		Learning outcomes: All pupils will ..... Most pupils will ..... Some pupils will	
Links to prior learning: *Insert here any information from your assessment data*		Links to cross-curricular learning: Literacy Numeracy PSHE Citizenship Other	
Homework:			

Time	Activities (teacher/pupil)	Assessment opportunities *Indicate <u>how</u> you will assess and <u>what</u> you will assess during the lesson*	Resources /Notes
	Starter:		
	Learning episodes:		
	Plenary:		

Figure 11.1 Lesson plan pro-forma

Activity 11.4   Assessment criteria

Assessment criteria should be specific to the task so you will need to adapt National Curriculum level descriptions or examination grade criteria. Think of one lesson or unit of work that you have taught, or will be teaching, to a Year 9 group and use the table on p. 100 to plan detailed assessment criteria against the National Curriculum level descriptions. (You will find some guidance for this activity on the NC in Action website www.ncaction.org.uk.) Make sure that you identify clearly what pupils will need to do to achieve each of the levels *in this specific activity*.

N.B. level descriptions are not usually used to assess one specific activity, but you may use them to guide you in this activity.

Activity 11.4 *continued*

Assessment opportunity (Indicate what pupils will do, or produce, as the assessment evidence)	
A level 4 answer will include/show	
A level 5 answer will include/show	
A level 6 answer will include/show	

Source: Adapted from DfES (2004b)

Peer assessment is a good introduction to self-assessment. Pupils will again need guiding, providing a template or framework for self-assessment helps. With practice, pupils will then learn to do the task autonomously.

It is helpful to share your expectations with pupils too. As well as giving pupils the learning objectives for the lesson you should talk to them about any assessments that you will be undertaking and discuss what you expect the outcomes to be – this helps pupils to prepare to meet your expectations.

SUMMATIVE ASSESSMENT

Although the emphasis may have changed, summative assessment is still an important part of the educational process with end-of-unit tests, Key Stage 3 teacher assessments and national examinations. You can use summative assessments as AfL in the following ways:

- using the data from summative assessments such as end-of-unit or KS2 and KS3 tests to inform your own planning;

- using the NC levels or examination grade criteria to help pupils self-assess. This may require you to reword the descriptions so that pupils better understand them.
- asking pupils to review the grade achieved in summative assessment to set their own learning targets.

When preparing pupils for summative assessments, such as examinations, it helps their learning if you ensure that they know and understand the assessment criteria and what they have to do to meet them. This means that you will need to be familiar with any summative tests undertaken in your school and with the examination requirements for Year 11 and Year 13 pupils.

HOW DOES AfL HELP PUPILS?

Research (Black and Wiliam 1998; Black *et al.* 2002) has shown that AfL helps to motivate pupils and contributes to effective teaching; it does this in a number of ways. We have already discussed the role of peer and self-assessment and the importance of effective feedback. These strategies will help pupils set targets for their own learning.

Target-setting involves pupils in deciding what level/grade they want to achieve and what they have to do to achieve it, and this can help with motivation. Target-setting can be based on examination grades, National Curriculum levels or the school's own criteria. A student teacher was observed conducting a textiles lesson in which all the pupils were at different stages in their work; she began the lesson by giving each pupil a Post-It note on which they wrote their own target for that lesson. The target had to state what the pupil would have done by the end of the lesson, *and* what they would have learnt; these were then reviewed at the end of the lesson and prepared pupils for the next lesson.

Form tutors are often involved in target-setting with pupils, with time set aside to discuss academic progress with pupils, set targets and record these in Pupil Progress Files. You may want to explore the role of the form tutor in relation to AfL in your own school.

There is also some evidence (Ofsted 2003) that good assessment practices can contribute to raising the attainment of boys, who are currently considered to be under-performing. Ofsted reports that boys respond well to teachers who have high expectations, set short-term targets and provide feedback that focuses on how they can improve; these are all aspects of good assessment practice. There is further guidance on gender and achievement on the DfES website: www.standards.dfes.gov.uk.

In order for AfL to be effective, it is also crucial that you keep records of assessments and targets, these can inform your own planning and be used to inform pupils, other teachers and parents/carers. Record keeping is discussed in more detail in *Learning to Teach Design and Technology in the Secondary School* (Owen-Jackson 2007).

MANAGING ASSESSMENT FOR LEARNING

It would appear from this chapter that you will spend all your time planning for assessment, assessing and providing feedback – but, of course, this cannot be the case. Assessment is only one part of effective teaching and you have to ensure that your assessment practice is manageable. There may be answers to this within your school, for example, some school policies require marking of pupils' work at regular intervals, but staggered so that over a period of time all classes are covered. Others ways of making assessment for learning manageable include undertaking assessment during lesson time – using some of the methods described above such as making notes as you observe pupils' working, noting evidence from starter/plenary activities and involving pupils in assessment – peer and self-assessment activities can be conducted in lesson time or as homework activities. Where ICT systems are used, these may take some time to become familiar with but can be time-saving in the longer term.

E-PORTFOLIOS

There has been some discussion of the use of e-portfolios as assessment tools. The rapid development of technologies means that electronic 'tools' such as PDAs, mobile phones, smart phones and tablet computers can be used to capture design sources, such as photographs or voice-recorded notes, for sketching with written or voice-recorded annotations, to record work as it develops and to share work and ideas with others. It is also possible that e-portfolios can then be submitted directly to the Award Board for assessment. However, the current availability and use of ICT in schools mean that these possibilities are not yet in practice but a research project is currently investigating their use (Kimbell 2006). This is an area of assessment practice that is likely to change over the next few years and you will need to keep abreast of developments through reading professional literature and accessing websites. A useful website for AfL is The Research Informed Practice Site on the DfES standards website (type 'research informed practice' into the search engine).

SUMMARY

This chapter has focussed on developing your practice in assessment for learning and you should now be familiar with why this is done and some methods that you can use in the classroom. Remember, though, that the importance of assessment is its role in planning and to improve pupils' learning, so any assessment activity you undertake should contribute to these.

REFERENCES

Assessment Reform Group (1999) *Assessment for Learning: Beyond the Black Box*, Cambridge: University of Cambridge, Faculty of Education

Black, P., Harrison, C., Lee, C., Marshall, B. and Wiliam, D. (2002) *Working inside the Black Box: Assessment for Learning in the Classroom*, London: King's College

Black, P. and Wiliam, D. (1998) *Inside the Black Box: Raising Standards through Classroom Assessment*, London: King's College

DfEE/QCA (2000) *Design and Technology: A Scheme of Work for Key Stage 3*, London: QCA www.standards.dfee.gov.uk/schemes

DfES (2004a) *Key Stage 3 National Strategy Foundation Subjects: Design and Technology Framework and Training Materials*, London: HMSO www.standards.dfes.gov.uk

DfES (2004b) *Key Stage 3 National Strategy Assessment for Learning*, London: DfES

DfES/QCA (1999) *The National Curriculum for England Design and Technology*, London: HMSO www.nc.uk.net

Kimbell, R. (2006) 'The e-scape project', presentation at Design and Technology Association Conference, University of Wolverhampton, July 2006

Ofsted (2003) *Boys' Achievement in Secondary Schools*, HMI 1659, London: Ofsted www. ofsted.gov.uk

Owen-Jackson, G. (2000) *Learning to Teach Design and Technology in the Secondary School*, London: Routledge

FURTHER READING

Assessment of Performance Unit (1991) *The Assessment of Performance in Design and Technology*, London: SEAC

WEBSITES

www.ncaction.org.uk
www.standards.dfes.gov.uk

Chapter 12 Planning your teaching

GWYNETH OWEN-JACKSON

INTRODUCTION

When you think about 'lesson planning' it appears to be easy – decide what you are going to teach, write it down, list the resources you will need, make sure it will fit into the time slot – done! However, *effective* lesson planning requires a little more thought. In fact, I would go further and suggest that lesson planning is a complex and creative activity, but one that is crucial to effective teaching and pupil learning.

Writing a lesson plan is a little like putting together the pieces of a jigsaw, where all the small pieces interlock to make a coherent picture. As with learning to do jigsaws, though, you may need to focus first of all on getting the main pieces in place before you can put in the final pieces that make up the picture. The complexity of planning means that this chapter could fill the whole book – but it focuses on helping you to plan lessons while in school and refers you to other readings where necessary. *Learning to Teach Design and Technology in the Secondary School* (Owen-Jackson, 2007) discusses in detail the reasons for planning lessons and the elements that comprise a lesson plan.

By the end of this chapter you should:

- be aware of the range of factors involved in lesson planning;
- be able to write appropriate learning objectives and learning outcomes;
- be able to write lesson plans that address all the necessary elements;
- have considered ways of planning for creativity in your lessons.

INDIVIDUAL LESSON PLANS

When you begin teaching you are likely to be asked to plan single lessons. This is short-term planning, so I start with these; although as you will see later single lesson plans are usually derived from medium-term and long-term plans.

Before you can begin to plan any lesson you need to be in possession of a great deal of knowledge. Some of this knowledge you will acquire through your training and through reading and you will be able to apply it to all lesson plans; other knowledge is specific to the lesson to be taught, such as the subject content and the pupils, and you will need to acquire this each time you plan a new topic or teach a new class. Activity 12.1 will help you to think about this.

Activity 12.1 Auditing your knowledge for lesson planning

For each lesson that you plan, use the table below as a checklist before you begin planning. If possible, discuss the completed table with your tutor or mentor to ensure that you have identified areas for development and how these might be addressed.

Questions to consider	What you already know	Areas for development, and action points
Subject knowledge – do you have detailed knowledge of the subject or topic?		See Chapters 2–6 in this book and *Learning to Teach Design and Technology in the Secondary School* (Owen-Jackson, 2007)
National Curriculum requirements for Design and Technology – do you know what pupils are expected to be taught, and at what level?		See *Learning to Teach Design and Technology in the Secondary School*
Curriculum initiatives and cross-curricular requirements – are you aware of government initiatives and how these impact on teaching D&T in your school?		See Chapter 9
Cross-curricular requirements (PSHE, citizenship, literacy, numeracy, key skills) –do you know how Design and Technology can contribute to these?		See Chapter 9
Learning styles – do you know *the* about the different ways in which pupils learn?		See *Learning to Teach in Secondary School* Capel et al. (1995) and *Learning to Teach Design and Technology in the Secondary School* (Owen-Jackson 2007)

Activity 12.1 *continued*

Teaching strategies – do you know a range of teaching strategies and when each one might be appropriate?		See *Learning to Teach Design and Technology* in *the Secondary School*
The pupils – do you know the pupils to be taught?; their previous experiences and levels of attainment?		
The pupils – are you aware of their individual needs, or any equality or inclusion issues? Does any pupil have an Individual Education Plan (IEP)?		See *Learning to Teach Design and Technology in the Secondary School* (Owen-Jackson 2007)
The learning environment – what resources are available to you? Do you need to consider health and safety issues? Is the learning environment appropriate and suitable?		See Chapter 8
Working as a team – do you need to take account of others in your planning? For example, will there be a teaching assistant, if so, what is his/her role and how can you plan jointly with the teaching assistant?		

Learning objectives and learning outcomes

The main piece of the lesson-planning jigsaw is knowing what the purpose of the lesson is – what do you want pupils to learn? This is not as simple a question as it seems and it can be difficult to state clearly and precisely what you expect but being clear and precise here will aid your planning.

I use the term 'learning objective' to describe what pupils will learn, elsewhere you may see it referred to as a lesson objective, teaching objective or a learning outcome. In Design and Technology learning objectives can relate to what pupils will *know* and what they will be able *to do*, so you could frame your objectives as:

- pupils will know . . .
- pupils will be able to . . .

Learning objectives and outcomes should be shared with pupils at the start of the lesson and one way of doing this is to refer to them as 'WALT' and 'WILF'; these acronyms stand for:

- We are learning to . . . this allows you to share the learning objectives with pupils.
- What I am looking for is . . . this allows you to share the learning outcomes.

You may find these terms used in your school as well as, or in place of, learning objectives and outcomes as they are from the Secondary National Strategy.

Learning objectives need to be set at an appropriate level of challenge in order to motivate pupils and prevent feelings of boredom or frustration. In order to plan appropriate learning objectives, you will need assessment data so that you know what level the pupils are working at and have knowledge of what they have done previously. You will eventually build this knowledge for yourself but initially you may need to ask your mentor. This idea is discussed further in *Learning to Teach Design and Technology in the Secondary School* (Owen-Jackson 2007).

You also need to plan ways of assessing whether or not pupils have learnt what you planned, I use the term 'learning outcome' to describe what the pupils produce as evidence of attainment of the learning objective. For example, your learning objective might be that the pupils 'will be able to write a specification for a product'. Lesson activities could include discussion of what a specification is and how it is used, you may have examples to show the pupils, and you could begin by compiling a specification as a whole-class activity before asking pupils to write a specification. The specification produced by each pupil would be the learning outcome as it would allow you to check individual understanding and attainment of the learning objective.

Be creative when planning outcomes, theoretical knowledge does not always have to be demonstrated by written worksheets, pupils could give an oral presentation, write a magazine article or information leaflet, they could present information graphically. Procedural knowledge could be demonstrated through what pupils do in a practical lesson or through producing a PowerPoint demonstration of a process, producing a flowchart or writing an instruction leaflet.

You should also plan assessment opportunities into your lesson so that you can monitor pupils' progress as the lesson proceeds, rather than finding out at the end that they totally misunderstood what you wanted! Assessment opportunities could include:

- short question-and-answer sessions or quiz sessions during the lesson;
- observations of pupils working;
- individual conversations with pupils;
- short activities in the lesson, such as asking pupils to summarise what they have done.

These assessment opportunities will indicate whether or not pupils are making the progress you intended and will allow you to intervene, if necessary, with individual pupils or the whole class before the final learning outcome is achieved.

The learning objectives are usually the same for all the class. You want them all to learn the same thing, but the outcomes will vary according to pupils' individual abilities and interests. For example, some pupils will be able to produce work beyond the expected level, a complex specification which takes account of a range of parameters, while others will achieve only the minimum level expected, a simple specification detailing only major aspects. Your lesson plan should indicate the different levels of outcome that you expect to see as this will allow you to plan for differentiated teaching and learning in the lesson. Differentiation is discussed in more detail in *Learning to Teach Design and Technology in the Secondary School*. (Owen-Jackson, 2007).

Activity 12.2 Learning objectives, pupil activities and learning outcomes

On the grid below match up suitable learning objectives, pupil activities and learning outcomes.

Learning objective	Possible pupil activity	Possible learning outcome
Pupils will know the properties of cotton, linen, silk and wool		
		A poster showing how mechanisms change motion
	Pupils to work in groups to produce a batch of savoury scones	
		A simple circuit with components and wires securely soldered
Pupils will be able to select and safely use appropriate equipment		
	Practical investigations to explore the uses of modern materials	

This activity will, hopefully, have alerted you to the differences between planning for:

* what pupils will learn – the learning objective;
* what they will do – pupil activity in the lesson;
* what they will produce to demonstrate learning – the learning outcome.

Selecting appropriate learning objectives and outcomes requires thought but it can be creative and is the foundation for effective teaching and learning. After fitting the learning objectives and outcomes jigsaw pieces together, you can then plan activities that will allow pupils to attain these, and these will constitute the main part of the lesson content.

Planning pupil activities

The Key Stage 3 National Strategy developed the idea of the 'three-part lesson', that is a lesson that has:

1 a starter activity;
2 learning episodes;
3 a plenary session.

Starter activities are short (5–10 minutes) and designed to help pupils quickly focus on the lesson. Plenary activities are used to summarise and monitor learning and to prepare pupils for what comes next. Ideas for starter and plenary activities can be found in the Key Stage 3 National Strategy materials for Design and Technology (DfES 2004) and elsewhere. They include:

- *Line-ups* – where pupils line up in a continuum to demonstrate their position on a particular issue, such as recycling.
- *Word association* – where words chosen at random from a piece of text are used to generate or explore ideas.
- *Mind-mapping*
- *Sequencing* – where pupils are given cards which describe a process and are asked to put them in the correct order.
- *Matching pairs* – where half the class are given cards that contain a word and half are given cards that contain a definition, pupils have to find their 'partner'.
- *Traffic lights* – where you ask questions and pupils indicate whether they fully know the answer, are not sure or don't know through holding up green, amber or red cards.
- *Key points* – pupils are asked to name three key questions, or things that they have learnt in the lesson.

Teachers have also developed their own starter and plenary activities and you may find plenty of interesting activities in your own school. Use Activity 12.3 to help you keep a record of these.

Activity 12.3 Starter and plenary activities

Observe a range of lessons in your school, not just in Design and Technology but in as many different subjects as possible. Note below any starter or plenary activities that you could use in your Design and Technology lessons.

Note here starter or plenary activities that you have observed and which you could use in Design and Technology

---

Activity 12.3 *continued*

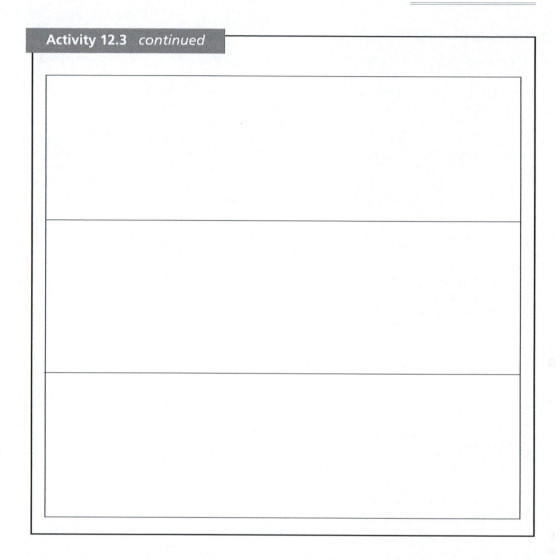

It is tempting to think that in busy Design and Technology lessons there is not enough time for starter and plenary activities but as they are intended to be short and quick you should be able to build them into most lessons. Try to plan a starter and/or plenary in lessons where they will be appropriate.

Planning practical work

Much of the work that takes place in Design and Technology is practical, whether it is pupils manufacturing a product or prototype, experimenting with materials or conducting product analysis. Planning practical work needs careful consideration. Points you should consider include:

- Do you know what each pupil will be doing in the lesson?
- Has each pupil got a target for the lesson?
- Do you know what resources will be required, and have you planned for and prepared them?
- Have you considered health and safety, and undertaken a risk assessment if necessary?
- Have you planned for any demonstration work that may be needed?
- How will you monitor the work of each pupil?

Planning to use ICT

ICT in its many forms is used in many Design and Technology lessons. In your plans consider whether or not ICT would help pupils' learning, for example, could they use the Internet for research? Is there a software program that would help with design work? Could they use PowerPoint for a presentation rather than produce a written folder?

If ICT would benefit pupils' learning, then your lesson plan needs to consider how this will be integrated, for example, is the required hardware and software available in the room or do you need to book space elsewhere? Are there sufficient resources for the number of pupils? Are you familiar with the software? What will you do if the ICT hardware or software doesn't work? (See Chapter 8 in this book and *Learning to Teach Design and Technology in the Secondary School* (Owen-Jackson 2000) for more on ICT in the subject.)

Planning for creativity

Creativity is an important aspect of Design and Technology and there are two aspects to consider in your planning – one is making your own teaching creative, the other is to plan activities to encourage and support pupils' creativity. Both of these are discussed in Chapter 7 in this book, but do consider during the planning process ways of introducing variety and interest into your lessons.

Putting it all together

In order to complete a single lesson plan there are a number of stages that you need to go through. The checklist below will help.

Activity 12.4   Lesson planning checklist

If you have to plan a lesson in your school, then use that lesson for this task, if not, then think of a lesson that you have observed and how it might have been planned. Use the checklist below for each lesson that you plan.

	Do you know the contextual information – the date of the lesson, its time, which room you will use, the year group, the number of pupils in the group, if any pupils have special needs?
	What is the topic of the lesson? Are you confident with this?
	What have the pupils previously done on this? What do they already know? What did they do last lesson?
	What do they need to know or do now? Plan the learning objectives.
	How will you know whether or not they have achieved the learning objectives? Plan the learning outcomes, remembering that pupils will produce the outcomes at different levels.
	What activities will allow the pupils to achieve the learning outcomes? Plan the learning and teaching activities, include an appropriate starter activity and plenary.
	Are there any National Curriculum or examination specification requirements that you need to take account of?
	Are there any cross-curricular initiatives that you need to take account of – literacy, numeracy, key skills, citizenship – or can build in to this topic?

Activity 12.4 *continued*

	What individual pupil needs do you need to plan for? Consider pupils with special needs or Individual Education Plans, consider pupils of different abilities and the needs of boys and girls.
	How long will the lesson last? Consider the timing of activities, is this appropriate and reasonable?
	What is the learning environment? Consider resources available, do you need to prepare or pre-book any resources? Do you need to undertake a risk assessment, have you planned for health and safety?
	Will you have the support of a teaching assistant or technician? Consider his/her role in the lesson and plan to discuss the lesson plan with him/her.
	Are you required to plan homework?
	What will pupils do next lesson? Can you link that in to this lesson?

Figure 12.1 gives you an example of what a completed single lesson plan might look like. This lesson plan has been completed to help you insert products appropriate to your own specialist focus area.

Planning, however time-consuming, is not the final stage – before the lesson you may have to do some preparation, for example, checking equipment/resources or practising a demonstration. This is discussed in *Learning to Teach Design and Technology in the Secondary School* (Owen-Jackson 2007).

MEDIUM-TERM AND LONG-TERM PLANNING

The single lessons you plan should be derived from schemes of work developed by the Design and Technology department. These are medium-term plans and usually cover a half-term or term. Examples of schemes of work for Design and Technology have been produced by the Qualifications and Curriculum Authority, see www.standards.dfee.gov.uk/schemes.

Schemes of work are, in turn, derived from long-term plans which provide only an outline of what will be covered; they usually arise from the National Curriculum or examination specification and cover a whole year or key stage. An example of a long-term plan for Design and Technology is given in the Key Stage 3 National Strategy materials (DfES 2004). Owen-Jackson (2007) describes medium- and long-term planning in more detail.

LESSON EVALUATIONS

When you begin to plan and teach your own lessons, some will go really well and you will feel pleased and rewarded, some will not go so well and you may feel deflated. What is important in both these cases is that you take some time to think through *why* a lesson went well, or not. It is likely that you will be required by your training institution to produce written lesson evaluations, and these will be important evidence to show how your own thinking and learning is developing.

In the early stages your lesson evaluations are likely to focus on what you did in the lesson, so think about:

- Were your subject knowledge and skills appropriate?
- How well planned was the lesson, did you plan in sufficient detail and think about all circumstances?

Date ....   **Lesson** ...1 of 8 ...11.30 – 12.30   **Room** ...G4 ..
Scheme of Work ...design and make an environmentally-friendly product
Topic ...product analysis ....
Class ...9JM – 23 pupils – 11 boys/12 girls mixed ability, no IEPs ....
Current NC levels: majority 4, PB/BR 3, PM/NR 5+
NR to sit at front – PM could be extended

Links to NC (Key Stage 3): 1a, 1c, 3c
(this refers to the National Curriculum for England 1999)

Cross-curricular learning:
Literacy – technical vocabulary (specific materials, appropriate terminology)
Citizenship – the world as a global community 1i, political, moral, social issues 2a

Previous learning:
Product analysis previously undertaken, no sustainable work done yet

Learning objectives:	**Learning outcomes:**
• Pupils to know that existing products can form the basis of new product development • Pupils to know how product design links to environmental/sustainable issues • Pupils to develop at least three criteria to inform their own product specification	• Star diagrams and product analysis sheets (showing criteria for analysis) • Criteria for own product

Timing	Lesson activities	Assessment opportunities	Resources/Notes
11.30	Starter: Line-ups – pupils to line up according to how much of their personal waste they recycle e.g. water bottles, Coke cans, paper, clothing	Some indication of existing knowledge/interest in ESD issues	Make sure there is enough space in the room for the line
11.40	PowerPoint on the importance of recycling to the environment/ sustainability issues	Questions/discussion will indicate current level of understanding	Have this set up and ready
11.50	In groups Hand out boxes to each table, each with 3–4 products in. Each group to analyse at least two products and record how recyclable they are and how environmentally-friendly.	Walk round and observe/listen to discussions	Have group lists ready Have product boxes ready Hand out worksheets for recording analysis
12.10	Whole-class, brainstorm what makes products recyclable/ non-recyclable? So what criteria would be important if a product was to be recyclable? Each pupil write down as many as they can think of.	Monitor level of knowledge/ understanding	Record on board (save for next lesson)
12.25	Homework Look around at home, your daily life, and consider one product that you use that could be made recyclable. Or, think of how people could be encouraged to recycle more, e.g. a convenient way to recycle plastic drinking cups. This will form the start of next lesson as they each develop a design brief.		Have this prepared on board – pupils to write homework in book, monitor this as they write

Figure 12.1 Sample lesson plan

- How well prepared was the lesson?
- What teaching strategies did you use, how successful were these?
- What did you say and how did you conduct yourself in the lesson?
- Was the timing right for the activities?

As you become more practised in the classroom, your evaluations should aim to focus on what the pupils learnt, so you will need to ask yourself questions such as:

- How appropriate were the learning objectives and outcomes? Were they sufficiently challenging?
- Were the pupils engaged throughout the lesson? Were there times when they had nothing to do or too much to do? Did the pupils understand what they were asked to do?
- What did the pupils learn from this lesson? How do you know?

Consider for each of these questions how you could improve if you were to teach the same lesson again.

SUMMARY

Lesson planning is a skill that improves the more you practise it, so I would suggest that you write plans for all your lessons. This will be time-consuming, it has been said that a one-hour lesson requires two hours of planning, but the time spent will be paid back in the classroom, where lessons should run more smoothly and pupil learning will be more evident. Don't worry if your mentor does not appear to be planning lessons, experienced teachers have 'plans-in-memory' (Calderhead 1984, p. 69), their years of experience and knowledge of the pupils have allowed them to shortcut detailed planning. In time, you too will be able to shorten your own planning but for now it is important that you produce detailed plans in order to demonstrate, to yourself, and others, your thinking and learning.

Lesson planning is a complex activity and there are many things that you need to know and think about in order to plan effectively. This chapter has introduced some of these considerations, but you will need to bring together your knowledge from different aspects of your training and experience in order to fully develop your planning skills.

REFERENCES

Calderhead, J. (1984) *Teachers' Classroom Decision Making*, Eastbourne: Holt, Rinehart and Winston

DfEE/QCA (1999) *Design and Technology: The National Curriculum for England* London: HMSO, www.nc.uk.net

DfES (2002) *Key Stage 3 National Strategy: Training Materials for the Foundation Subjects*, London: HMSO

DfES (2004) *Key Stage 3 National Strategy Foundation Subjects: Design and Technology Framework and Training Materials*, London: HMSO

Owen-Jackson, G. (2000) *Learning to Teach Design and Technology in the Secondary School*, London: Routledge

QCA/DfEE (2000) *Design and Technology: A Scheme of Work for Key Stage 3*, London: QCA

FURTHER READING

Most books on teacher training include a section on planning, two that are recommended are:

Bourdillon, H. and Storey, A. (eds) (2002) *Aspects of Teaching and Learning in Secondary Schools Perspectives on Practice*, London: RoutledgeFalmer/The Open University. Chapter 5, 'Planning for teaching and learning'.

Brooks, V., Abbott, I. and Bills, L. (2004) *Preparing to Teach in Secondary Schools*, Maidenhead: Open University Press, Chapter 5, 'Planning for learning'.

Part 3 Continuing your professional development

Chapter 13 Your professional development

ROWAN TODD AND JOHN LEE

INTRODUCTION

Whichever route you choose for your initial training, you will need to seek out opportunities to extend your personal capability in Design and Technology and combine this with the academic and professional skills needed to meet the wider demands of being a teacher.

You will have the opportunity through school placements to put your knowledge into action in a professional context and develop the teaching competences outlined in *Qualifying to Teach* (TTA 2002).[1] During your initial training, it is important to maintain a record of your developing capability in ways that will allow you to reflect on your progress and establish appropriate targets.

Later, during your induction period and in the early years of teaching, you will need to continue the process of identifying priorities for future professional development and consider how these change over time. The professional development process is a continuum that enables you to take responsibility for your own progress during initial training and throughout your subsequent teaching career. This chapter will introduce you to strategies that are designed to support you in managing your continuing professional development.

By the end of this chapter you should be able to:

- engage in a cycle of needs analysis, target setting and action planning to develop an awareness of the skills and knowledge you will require to become an effective teacher of Design and Technology;
- reflect on your professional practice and recognise the need for continuing professional development beyond completion of your initial training;
- demonstrate an understanding of the professional standards that you will be judged against at various stages in your career.

MANAGING YOUR DEVELOPMENT DURING YOUR INITIAL TRAINING

During the initial phase of your training, you will become familiar with a range of materials that outline the subject requirements for Design and Technology, such as the National Curriculum Programmes of Study (DfES/QCA 1999), the DATA fields of knowledge (DATA 2003) and public examinations specifications. These will help you to gain an understanding of the skills, knowledge and capability you will need to become an effective teacher of Design and Technology.

The Design and Technology Association – the professional association for teachers of Design and Technology – suggests that you should be confident to teach in two specialist

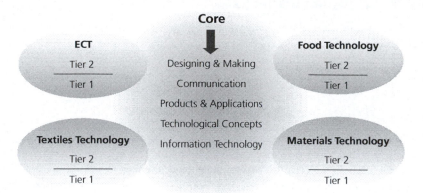

Figure 13.1 Focus areas within Design and Technology

focus areas of Design and Technology at KS3 and one specialist area at KS4 and beyond. This is illustrated by Figure 13.1.

Whatever your previous experience, you will have particular strengths and aspirations in relation to teaching Design and Technology. One of the first things you will need to think about is the relationship between your present capability and the skills and knowledge you need for teaching. This in turn will enable you to set targets for future development and determine a programme of study that is tailored to your individual needs.

WHERE ARE YOU NOW?

Your subject knowledge will continue to develop throughout the course, and when you are teaching, and it is important to monitor and record this progression. There are a number of stages to this, as a starting point you will need to find out where you are now. Carrying out a 'subject knowledge audit', as described in *Learning to Teach Design and Technology in the Secondary School* (Owen-Jackson 2007) is an effective way of doing this. You will need to consider the integration of what you already know with the skills, knowledge and values that you will need to acquire to become an effective practitioner of Design and Technology education.

Figure 13.2 shows how students at one university made use of radar diagrams to create a visual record of their progress in developing their subject knowledge.

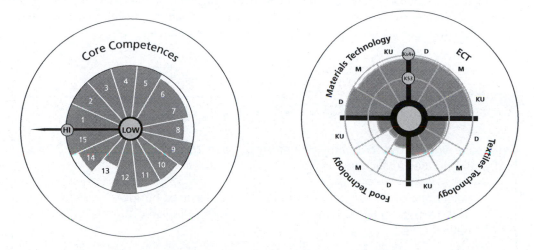

Figure 13.2 Recording subject knowledge

MONITORING YOUR PROGRESS

Once you have established where you are and gained an understanding of where you need to be, you will need to choose a method of monitoring and recording your development. Methods you might consider include compiling a reflective journal or creating a digital/e-portfolio.

Compiling a reflective journal

Writing analytically about your experiences with the purpose of developing a greater understanding of teaching and learning is a powerful strategy. This type of writing, often referred to as 'reflective writing', can be used to make connections between theory and practice; concepts and observations; reading and experience; beliefs and behaviour; thoughts and feelings; old knowledge and new knowledge; between yourself and other students; and between yourself and more experienced colleagues.

Compiling a reflective journal will enable you to consider your professional development in a systematic way. It can help you to identify personal strengths and weaknesses and assist you in tracking your personal development, both in the context of your subject knowledge and the ability to apply this within the teaching environment.

There is no one right way to organise and write a journal. However, as it is likely that your journal will be read by others, it will help to structure it in a way that makes it simple for the reader to understand what you are trying to convey through your journal entries. Here are some ways you may wish to consider:

- *as a personal learning journey*: documenting an evolving understanding of teaching and learning both in your training and professional practice in schools; for example by selecting one or two significant situations that occurred during any given week and describing in detail what happened, how you felt about it, and what you have learned;
- *in terms of issues*: an example might be to take a topic you have been studying, something you have read in the literature or an incident that occurred as part of your teaching and learning and use this as a basis for reflection;
- *as a series of critical reflections*: on events that you have encountered, for example, you might want to consider a noteworthy incident that took place in your classroom and record your thoughts on the matter.

Whichever structure you choose, and it could well be a combination of all of these, your writing needs to demonstrate active and reflective engagement in the issues and ideas you encounter. It is important to remember that the journal is a tool through which you can reflect upon your student teaching experience and grow as a beginning teacher.

Activity 13.1 Reflective writing

Choose one of the following as a starting point to reflect on aspects of your development as a teacher:

1   Select one or two significant situations that occurred during any given week and describe in detail what happened, how you feel about it and what you have learned.

Activity 13.1 *continued*

2   Take a topic you have been studying, something you have read in the literature or an incident that occurred as part of your teaching and learning and use the following questions to guide your reflection:

    (a) What is the current problem or issue? Describe the context.
    (b) How is it related to other issues?
    (c) Who or what could help to further your understanding?
    (d) How does the issue connect with aspects of your practice?
    (e) What are the teaching and learning principles involved?

3   Consider a noteworthy incident that took place in your classroom:

    (a) Describe the incident as objectively as possible.
    (b) What were the assumptions that you made?
    (c) Is there another way to see this incident?
    (d) How would your pupils explain this incident?
    (e) How do the two explanations compare?

CREATING AND MAINTAINING AN E-PORTFOLIO

Creating and maintaining a portfolio in electronic format offers an exciting and innovative way of evidencing your personal capability in Design and Technology. It will enable you to present information in various formats such as text, images, videos, etc.

An e-portfolio is a flexible tool that can provide continuity as you progress through the different phases of your career. It may include some or all of the following:

- personal information including a CV;
- subject knowledge and prior experience;
- teaching experience;
- extra-curricular interests;
- your own philosophy about the nature and purpose of Design and Technology;
- career aspirations.

Presentation packages such as PowerPoint or website authoring software such as Front Page or Dream Weaver can be effective vehicles for compiling an e-portfolio. Figure 13.3 shows sample pages from an e-portfolio.

MANAGING PROFESSIONAL DEVELOPMENT IN THE EARLY YEARS OF YOUR CAREER

Your development as a teacher does not stop at the end of your period of initial training but will carry on throughout your career. During your first three terms as a newly qualified teacher, known as your induction period, you will be given the opportunity to negotiate a programme of training and support which will help you integrate into your new school and provide the foundations for your future professional development.

During your induction period, you will be expected to continue to meet the standards for the award of QTS as well as demonstrate the ability to meet a set of nationally agreed induction standards.[2] Your induction programme will be based in part on targets you have

---

Activity 13.2 Starting an electronic portfolio

Before creating an e-portfolio you will need to collate information that is to be included. Gather the appropriate information under the following headings:

1 **Prior experience**

   (a) academic – record and review your previous education and learning;
   (b) employment – record details of your employment experience including paid/unpaid/voluntary work.

2 **Personal interests**
   Record information about any relevant interests, hobbies, membership of clubs/societies, sporting activities, etc.

3 **Subject knowledge**

   (a) identify your strengths as a beginning teacher of Design and Technology;
   (b) identify areas you need (or would like) to develop further.

4 **Professional perspective**

   (a) document your personal philosophy on the nature and purpose of Design and Technology;
   (b) consider your personal career aspirations.

5 **Teaching experience**
   Record examples of successful school-based practice in which you have been involved.

---

identified through your career entry and development profile (CEDP – see http://www.tda. gov.uk/teachers/induction/cedp.aspx and http://www.tda.gov.uk/teachers/induction/ cedp/cedpresources/resourcestp1.aspx) and tailored to your individual needs. It will usually involve you in working under the guidance of more experienced teachers, visiting other schools and taking part in formal training events and courses. At the end of your induction period you will be assessed against the induction standards.

After induction, the next accredited benchmark for teachers is performance threshold. The aim of the performance threshold is to encourage and reward good teaching. To satisfy the performance threshold standards you will have to demonstrate that you have a thorough and up-to-date knowledge of the teaching of your subject and are able to take account of wider curriculum developments which are relevant to your professional work. There is an expectation that you will have taken responsibility for your own professional development and that this has resulted in demonstrable improvements in your teaching and in your contribution to the policies and aspirations of the school.

The performance threshold only applies to experienced teachers, but the standards can be used by any teacher as a tool for reviewing practice in their early years of teaching and they give you a goal to work towards.

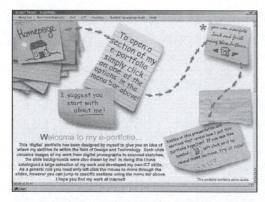
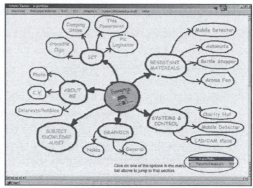
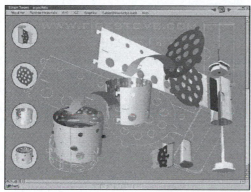
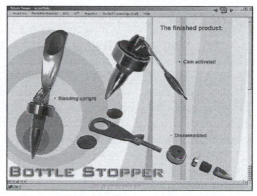
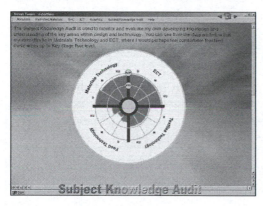
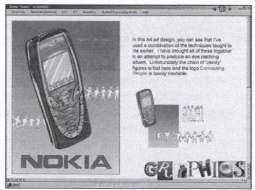

Figure 13.3 Sample pages from an e-portfolio

Activity 13.3 Understanding the Induction Standards

Obtain a copy of *The Induction Support Programme for Newly Qualified Teachers*, reference: DfES/0458/2003 (available at www.teachernet.gov.uk). Look at the Guidance document and ensure that you are familiar with:

- roles and responsibilities
- the Induction Standards.

CONTINUING PROFESSIONAL DEVELOPMENT (CPD)

During your early years in teaching your performance will continue to be monitored and discussed on a regular basis as part of the continuous cycle of appraisal that now operates in most schools. During this process you will usually work with experienced colleagues to identify your achievements and aspirations prior to setting targets and specifying your continuing professional development (CPD) needs.

CPD provides a means to ensure that your career is kept up to date and you remain well prepared to take advantage of opportunities for career progression. A comprehensive range of CPD and in service training opportunities are available to teachers from within the school community and through external bodies such as the local authority, higher education institutions, subject and professional associations and award boards.

CAREER PROGRESSION

Teaching offers excellent opportunities for career progression, both within and beyond the classroom. In addition to progression to roles of responsibility within the subject department, the Excellent Teacher scheme (ET) and Advanced Skills Teacher (AST) programme offer further career opportunities for excellent practitioners who wish to remain committed to the classroom. National standards for these two roles were introduced in September 2006 and, like the performance threshold standards, these will help you to review your progress and plan your career development.

'Fast Track' is another scheme that identifies talented and committed teachers and gives them access to development opportunities and support to enable them to take on wider positions of responsibility in schools and the world of education.

Activity 13.4 Professional and career development

Obtain access to TeacherNet's dedicated *Professional and Career Development* online support tool, (http://www.teachernet.gov.uk/development/) which is designed to provide guidance on effective planning for career progression in teaching.
Familiarise yourself with the content in the sections headed:

- Career Pathways
- Starting Points
- Getting Equipped
- Mapping Your Route
- Keeping Track
- Filing Cabinet

Reflect on how they may be useful to you in considering your career development. Where appropriate, this information can be added to your reflective journal and/or e-portfolio.

The General Teaching Council for England also offer a route for career progression with their Teacher Learning Academy (TLA). In order to follow this route you need to have obtained Qualified Teacher Status and be registered with the GTCE. The TLA route allows you to plan your own professional development, based on researching and improving your classroom practice, and gain accreditation. Details of the scheme can be found on the GTCE website, www.gtce.org.uk.

In this chapter we have only considered your professional development as a Design and Technology teacher but there are, of course, many other aspects to your work in school. You may, for example, wish to develop the pastoral side of your work; CPD will still be important but you will undertake different courses and different routes.

And the educational environment will continue to change; the introduction of extended schools as part of the Every Child Matters agenda, the development of academies, the introduction of 14–19 Diplomas – all will impact on your work in school and it will be important that you keep your knowledge up to date on all educational matters.

SUMMARY

Part of the challenge of becoming an effective professional teacher is the willingness to take ownership of your own learning. To do this, you will need to continually monitor where you are and be prepared to set the agenda for your own development. This will have a number of benefits. You will be better able to refine your personal capability, to respond to changes in the curriculum and to seek out new challenges in your career. The cycle of action, review and target setting will form the cornerstone of your continuing professional development, both within your period of initial training and throughout your subsequent career in teaching. It will be hard work, but well worth it!

NOTES

1 This document will be updated with new standards for Qualifying to Teach commencing in 2007 and new standards for Induction year commencing 2008. New standards for performance threshold/senior teacher, excellent teacher and advanced skills teacher were introduced in 2006.
2 These standards will be updated with new standards for Qualifying to Teach commencing in 2007 and new ones for induction year commencing 2008. New standards for performance threshold/senior teacher, excellent teacher and advanced skills teacher will be introduced in 2006.

FURTHER READING

Boud, D., Keogh, R. and Walker, D. (1995) *Reflection: Turning Experience into Learning*, London: Kogan Page

Brookefield, S.D. (1995) *On Becoming a Critically Reflective Teacher*, San Francisco: Jossey Bass

DATA (2003) *Minimum Competences for Students to Teach Design and Technology in Secondary Schools*, Research Paper 4, Wellesbourne: DATA

DfEE/QCA (1999) *Design and Technology Key Stages 1 to 4*, London: HMSO

Schön, D. (1987) *Educating the Reflective Practitioner*, San Francisco: Jossey Bass

Teacher Training Agency (2002) *Qualifying to Teach: Professional Standards for Qualified Teacher Status and Requirements for Initial Teacher Training*, London: TTA

Index

Lightning Source UK Ltd.
Milton Keynes UK
26 January 2011

166362UK00006BA/2/P